CIRO
&
SAL'S
COOKBOOK

CIRO
&
SAL'S
COOKBOOK

Recipes, Tips and Lore from the
Acclaimed Chef of Provincetown's
Famous Italian Restaurant, Ciro & Sal's

by
CIRO COZZI
with Alethea Cozzi

THE STEPHEN GREENE PRESS
PELHAM BOOKS

THE STEPHEN GREENE PRESS / PELHAM BOOKS

Published by the Penguin Group
Viking Penguin, a division of Penguin Books USA Inc., 40 West 23rd Street,
    New York, New York 10010, U.S.A.
Penguin Books Ltd, 27 Wrights Lane, London W8 5TZ, England
Penguin Books Australia Ltd, Ringwood, Victoria, Australia
Penguin Books Canada Ltd, 2801 John Street, Markham, Ontario,
    Canada L3R 1B4
Penguin Books (N.Z.) Ltd, 182-190 Wairau Road, Auckland 10, New Zealand

Penguin Books Ltd, Registered Offices: Harmondsworth, Middlesex, England

First published in 1987 by Donald I. Fine, Inc.
Reprinted by special arrangement with Donald I. Fine, Inc.
This edition published by The Stephen Greene Press / Pelham Books in 1989
Distributed by Viking Penguin, a division of Penguin Books USA Inc.

10   9   8   7   6   5   4   3   2   1

Library of Congress Cataloging-in-Publication Data

Cozzi, Ciro.
      Ciro & Sal's cookbook.

      Reprint. Originally published: New York : D.I. Fine, ©1987
      Includes index.
      1. Cookery, Italian. 2. Ciro & Sal's (Restaurant)
   I. Cozzi, Alethea. II. Title. III. Title: Ciro and Sal's cookbook.
   TX723.C684   1989   641.5'09744'92   88-34762
   ISBN 0-8289-0734-X

Printed in the United States of America
Designed by Stanley S. Drate/Folio Graphics Co. Inc.
Produced by Unicorn Production Services, Inc.

To Al,
for thirty years of love and laughter,
and without whom this book
would never have come to pass.

Acknowledgments
from Ciro Cozzi

Thank you to Mel and Al for their patience and tenacity in seeing this dream to its realization.

Thank you to all the artists that have passed through our doors. And a special thanks to those who have so generously contributed their work and memories to this book.

A very special thanks to my wife, Patti, and to my family for their tolerance, support and hard work through the years.

And to my daughter Alethea, thank you, for without you this book would never have been completed.

CONTENTS

INTRODUCTION

For more than three decades, visitors and locals alike have been streaming to the Provincetown restaurant known as CIRO & SAL'S. Many of these visitors are artists, both well-known and little known, and, from the beginning, they have played a major role, both as employees and as patrons, in the creation of this unique restaurant. They have lent to it a special atmosphere and have helped to spread its reputation for delicious—and abundant—Italian food, throughout the world.

The restaurant was established in the early 1950s by Ciro Cozzi and Sal Del Deo, who were both artists. The dishes on the menu are not restricted to any particular region of Italy: There are dishes from the south, from Rome, and from the north. However, all of the food has one thing in common—the creative touch of Ciro himself, who endlessly samples and experiments, while always insisting on high quality, excellent taste and ample portions. Here, at last, is the cookbook which will give you all the recipes for the dishes on CIRO & SAL'S menu, plus many more created by Ciro and his daughter Alethea.

In recent years, an interest in good food has developed all over the United States, and ingredients once difficult or even impossible to obtain can now be found in nearly every large supermarket, or, certainly, in specialty food stores. The ingredients needed to make the recipes in this book are not unusual: There are no secret substances, no expensive or rare spices—just the highest quality ingredients available for creating exciting and delicious food.

The cooking techniques used are just as straightforward as the ingredients. You need not order special equipment or take a cooking course. CIRO & SAL'S cooking secrets are revealed in an easy-to-follow format designed for the home cook. The finished dishes you serve will be the same as those enjoyed by the countless thousands who list a visit to CIRO & SAL'S, along with the sea and sun, as one of Provincetown's main attractions.

The artist Al DiLauro, who first conceived the idea for this book, was a waiter at the restaurant for thirty years and, needless to say, a part of the family. Everyone on the staff, and, of course, Ciro himself, helped Al to prepare the recipes from the restaurant menu. Following his untimely death in 1985, Alethea took up where Al left off, completing the book he had envisioned.

What you will find here, besides the recipes, are the unusual and often funny stories of how this phenomenon known as CIRO & SAL'S came into being, and how its recipes were developed. Many, indeed most, of the stories revolve around the diverse groups of artists and eccentrics who have made CIRO & SAL'S of Provincetown so unique. To express their own special memories of the restaurant, several of the artists have contributed photographs, cartoons, drawings and prose. We thank them all.

So sit back, enjoy the story and share a good meal with friends.

PART

I

THE
HISTORY

THE FIFTIES

Bronx-born Ciro Cozzi and Sal DelDeo met in Provincetown in the summer of 1947. They were both young and had come to study under Henry Hensche, the renowned colorist. Ciro was fresh out of the army, and Sal, who hails from Providence, Rhode Island, was an art student at Vesper George in Boston. The two young men became friends and then roommates, and for a few summers they both studied with Hensche. Then they both moved away: Sal joined the army and Ciro traveled to Colorado to study fresco technique under Jean Charlot. By 1951 both men were back in Provincetown and looking for a way to finance their art.

During the first years, Ciro worked as a sandal maker and as a construction worker (among other things) to support himself, his new wife Ero, and his growing family. By 1952 their third child was beginning to walk, and, as no one would rent to a family with three lively children, Ciro knew he had to try to buy a house.

Irene Millington owned a house on Kiley Court (then known as Peter Hunt's Lane), which she wanted to sell for nine thousand dollars. Ciro loved the house, but the price made it too expensive for him. Irene agreed to lower the price to about eight thousand dollars and to accept a deposit of eleven hundred dollars. Now all Ciro had to do was to find the money for the down payment. Ciro's father, who thought that his son was out of his mind to settle in a small town "at the end of the Earth," refused to help him. Ciro's uncle Amedeo, however, heard about his predicament and gave—not loaned—Ciro the money, which Ciro did repay, little by little, over the years.

After his family was settled in the house, Ciro began to fix up the extra rooms in the house as rental apartments, but he couldn't decide what to do with the large dirt-floored basement. Then he came up with the idea of opening up an after-hours pizza restaurant for the

3

fishermen and artists of the town. Ciro approached all his friends with the proposition but all of them refused to become his partner, because they felt it would ruin their friendship. Finally he asked Sal—and Sal agreed. The partnership was based on the idea that Sal, who had wanted to be an opera singer, would be a singing waiter and Ciro would bring his restaurant "experience" to the enterprise. (It should be noted that neither proprietor had ever cooked, and Ciro's restaurant experience consisted of stints as a waiter and dishwasher, both jobs at which he had not excelled.)

The two young men felt that they could make it, but they were alone in their enthusiasm. Their friends laughed and said, "Who's going to go down an alley to eat in a dirt cellar?" Despite these objections, Ciro and Sal were determined to go ahead with their plans. With ingenuity, resourcefulness and sixty dollars contributed by Sal, they soon created a restaurant. Their stove (a discard of the Everbreeze restaurant) was found at the town dump; their ice box (the kind into which you actually put blocks of ice) came from fellow painter and friend Eddie Euler; the silverware, glasses, plates, etc., were all donated by friends. Sal's father Romolo, who was a tinsmith, made the sinks for the kitchen by nailing sheets of tin onto plywood frames; he was also able to fashion the lanterns for the dining room out of oil cans. Their plans were in full swing when they learned that Ciro's cousin in New York had not been able to buy the necessary pizza ovens—they were too expensive. Ciro and Sal quickly decided that their menu would feature sandwiches and omelets instead.

CIRO & SAL'S opened for business that June—it was an instant success. Soon it became impossible to control the crowds that gathered in the alley outside the restaurant until three o'clock in the morning. Ciro's neighbors complained, and the Board of Selectmen were going to withdraw the restaurant's permit. However, Bill White, a member of the board, felt that the restaurant should be given a second chance, and he convinced his fellow selectmen to allow the restaurant to remain open—but only until eleven-thirty in the evening. There was no alternative but to start serving dinners.

To play it safe, Ciro and Sal initially offered only the standard spaghetti with ragù and spaghetti with ragù and meatballs. The sauce was a family recipe, so they had no difficulty. But then they decided to get more adventurous and add chicken "al cacciatore," which they called Chicken el Capitano (no one knows why). They went to the local A & P, where they did their daily shopping, and, being short of money, bought the most inexpensive and largest "chicken" they could

Neo-classicists, post-impressionists, proto-cubists,
pseudo-symbolists, anti-abstractionists and even
unreconstructed dadists all agree:
Ciro's and Sal's Meatball Sandwiches
are MASTERPIECES

CIRO AND SAL'S
Down Peter Hunt's Lane
SERVING DINNERS FROM 5 P. M. ON

One of the earliest advertisements for Ciro & Sal's. Joe DeRocco wrote the copy.

find. Not realizing that there was a difference between chicken and fowl (which was what they had), they simply roasted the bird with peppers, wine and herbs. The first order for the new dish came into the kitchen that night. The customer who had ordered it was sitting directly in view of the open kitchen. As the two "chefs" watched, the unsuspecting man took his first bite and tried to chew it. Then he tried again, and again. Finally he gave up and called the waiter. "The flavor is wonderful, but it's impossible to chew it," he said. It was a lesson they would never forget: Use only the best ingredients available. This was the point when they also decided that they had better start calling Ciro's mother for advice.

That summer Sal met Josephine Couch. They were to be married in November and they wanted to hold the wedding reception in the restaurant. They decided to pave the dirt floor for the event. So, every day for a week, Josephine drove her Model A Ford to the back shore to get sand, while Ciro and Sal gathered stones, bricks, and other objects to place in the cement. Together they paved the floor, and to this day Josephine can still remember how her legs ached throughout the wedding ceremony.

The next summer a few veal dishes, one or two fish dishes, and a few more pastas were added to the menu. Business grew with each new summer season, but this still did not mean that the two artists could afford to paint all winter, so they had to take on odd carpentry jobs whenever possible.

From the moment it opened its doors, the restaurant was a haven for young artists. They came and sat on padded and not-so-padded nail kegs to wait patiently for their dinners. After they had finished eating, they would stay and pass the evening talking, playing music, singing and drinking the free coffee provided by the owners. And, as these artists sat, they would often doodle; and from these doodles were devised posters for the walls and poems for advertisements, as well as ideas for their own future works.

Napi Van Derek (current owner of Napi's Restaurant) was one of the restaurant's best public relations men. At the time, he worked on Al Avilar's *Dolphin I*, and he would extoll the virtues of CIRO & SAL'S to anyone who would listen. All the restaurant's regulars were in the same boat—they were all struggling, so each helped the other. Napi would later become the restaurant's head dishwasher and a member of the "Dishwashers' Hall of Fame." He still holds the title of "Worst Dishwasher," mainly because he never washed a dish himself; instead, he had a team of boys do the work for him.

In 1956, Moe Van Derek followed his brother Napi and became the restaurant's dishwasher. From dishwasher he became a busboy, later graduating to waiter. During this time, he also became an accomplished guitarist and often entertained the guests at the restaurant. Moe worked as a waiter until 1971, when he left to devote all of his time to music.

In 1955, when Ciro and Sal could first afford a cleanup person, they hired a young American history student named Irving Sandler. That summer at the restaurant, Sandler met most of the artists who hung out there; he later described it as a "germinal period" in his life. It was there that he met artist Angelo Ippolito, who got Sandler a job that winter as a sitter in New York's Tanager Gallery on Tenth Street. A year later, Sandler was writing reviews for *Art News* and continuing his graduate studies. He eventually published a book on the period, *The Triumph of American Painting: A History of Abstract Expressionism*, and has been a frequent contributor to art journals.

Sandler is now professor of Art History at State University of New York, Purchase. The following is an excerpt from his memoir reprinted from the catalog, "The Sun Gallery—An Exhibition at Provincetown Art Association and Museum—1981":

Provincetown itself enhanced "the dream." With its dunes, ocean, and sun, and its light—as Motherwell wrote, "exactly the same kind of light that Matisse loved or Miro loved or the Greek sculptors loved"—it was just the place to believe in unlimited horizons and a shining future. It was far enough removed from the "real" world for a young person to invent his or her identity in "life" and, if serious, to aspire to it in art.

And there was a great deal of leisure time. Those who could take a summer off in Provincetown either could afford to do so, or could easily earn enough to live by working part time. One summer, I managed by washing the kitchen floor every night after closing, and the refrigerator once a week, at the newly opened CIRO & SAL'S restaurant, and by sitting in the HCE Gallery daily during lunch hours to relieve Ivan Karp, who worked there. My work week was under fifteen hours. The following season, I shared the cellar of a fishing captain's house on the bay with a painter and a writer. We each paid $33.33 for the summer's rent.

It was a special time, not only for CIRO & SAL'S but also for Provincetown, which had become a haven for artists and craftsmen. Of the latter, perhaps the most famous is Peter Hunt. Kiley Court ("The Alley"), where the restaurant is located, was previously Peter Hunt's Lane. According to the Provincetown Art Association and Museum, which sponsored a show of Peter Hunt's work in 1982, "Mr. Hunt came to Provincetown in the early 1920s. He had just returned from Europe where, during World War I, he had been an ambulance driver. Mr. Hunt arrived in Provincetown with long blond hair, two Afghan dogs, a large black cape and a dwarf in attendance. He was known as 'Peter Lord Templeton Hunt.'"

Mr. Hunt was an antique dealer who had trained as a painter. Working in primitive designs—or what he called "peasant designs"— he painted furniture, kitchen utensils, chests of drawers, pepper mills and any other utilitarian object that caught his fancy. His designs began a grass-roots movement, and a following developed. His work and his shop became popular nationally through the books he wrote on his craft.

Peter Lord Templeton Hunt's real name was Frederick L. Schnitzer.

In the late fifties, Milton Avery rented a studio from Mr. Hunt across from "The Alley." It had a beautiful view of the bay and it is where Avery painted his best and largest canvases. He was able to have these large canvases stretched by Jim Forsberg (also an artist) at the Studio Shop, which was next door. To get the canvases into his studio, Avery had to throw a rope out of his window and pull them up from the street. The Studio Shop is still there, and Jim Forsberg is still a regular at CIRO & SAL'S.

In 1958 Ciro and Sal added another dining room to the restau-

Ciro at Ciro & Sal's, 1956. *Eat* painting by Angelo Ippolito.

rant and replaced the kegs with real chairs. The following year they were finally able to obtain a beer and wine license, previously denied them because of a town law stating that any establishment serving alcohol had to be at least five hundred feet from the nearest church. A Christian Science church stood four hundred and eighty feet away and held services once a week—in the summer only.

Until 1959 customers brought their own wine, usually a straw-covered bottle of Chianti. One evening, Henry Morgan, the comedian, had a reservation and was late. When he arrived with his companion and his bottle of Chianti, the hostess said that she had given his table away and he would have to wait. Mr. Morgan turned, smashed his bottle of wine on the patio and left.

Someone started the practice of hanging the empty bottles on the walls and from the ceiling. The bottles are there to this day.

THE SIXTIES

Before the start of the 1960 summer season, Sal left the restaurant to pursue his painting full-time. (Within three years, though, he would be back in the business, this time with a restaurant of his own on the west side of town.) Ciro's life, too, would be changing.

As if in prescient anticipation of what would happen throughout the country in the coming years, the 1960s in Provincetown got off to a turbulent start.

For thirty years, Harry Kemp, a regular at CIRO & SAL'S and the last of the Bohemians, lived in a shack on the dunes, which earned him the nickname, "Poet of the Dunes." Harry had shared the shack on the back shore at Peaked Hill with an unknown playwright who would one day read his one-act play, *Bound East for Cardiff,* to the Provincetown Players. The playwright's name was Eugene O'Neill. Harry, too, was a writer, and during his life he wrote and published countless poems as well as the novel, *Tramping on Life.*

When he could no longer make the walk from the dunes into town, Rose "Sunny" Tasha built Harry a cabin, or shack as it was known, on her property off Howland Street, within easy walking distance of CIRO & SAL'S. Harry spent many of his last evenings at the restaurant drinking coffee and wine.

Several months before Harry died, in August 1960, a friend from New York convinced him to become a Catholic. The only close local friend Harry had who was a practicing Catholic was Ciro Cozzi, so, in a quiet ceremony performed by the local priest, Father Duarte, Ciro became Harry's godfather.

Harry had often said that when he died he wanted to be cremated and have his ashes scattered over both Greenwich Village in New York City and the dunes in Provincetown. So when Harry died, Sunny wanted to carry out his wishes. The local lawyer, doctor, and others

10

argued that a Catholic could not be cremated; they wanted to see Harry buried and a monument erected to him. This feeling was so strong that Attorney Oswald Bald threatened to sue Sunny for everything she had if Harry was cremated. Sunny's daughter even had threats made against her.

Nonetheless, Sunny sent the body by hearse to the crematorium up the Cape. The local physician, Doctor Hiebert, called the state police and had the hearse intercepted. The body was then put on view at the funeral parlor. Sunny's two eldest children asked her, "If you can't carry out Harry's wishes, how are we ever going to believe you about anything?" Sunny contacted a judge who told her that everything was legally left to her, including Harry's remains. She was then able to follow Harry's wishes, thanks to help from Harry's friend Hudson Walker, who paid for the cremation.

A few days later, while Sunny was waiting on tables at CIRO & SAL'S, a small box was delivered to her. Dan Bernstein (who later became a successful photographer) was working as cashier that night and he kept the box behind the cash register for the evening. It was Harry's last visit to the restaurant.

Soon afterward a popular magazine offered to pay Sunny for the story. However, Hudson Walker persuaded her not to talk to the magazine, because his friend, Senator John F. Kennedy, was running for President and controversial Catholic stories would not help his campaign.

It should be noted that on the day that Harry died, all the lights on Cape Cod went out briefly—as if in recognition of his passing.

Two more incidents would upset the art community that year and would establish CIRO & SAL'S as the place for artists and the like to gather and discuss their views—and sometimes to plan action.

That year the Sun Gallery had an exhibition of monotypes by Tony Vevers. The police came and ordered the show closed, because they objected to the monotypes of nudes with pubic hair. Strategy sessions were held at CIRO & SAL'S. Art patron Hudson Walker came to the gallery's aid by retaining a lawyer, and Hans Hofmann, another restaurant regular, drafted a manifesto that was signed by some 146 artists and supporters. Finally a compromise was reached: The gallery would hang a half curtain on the window so that children passing by would not be able to see in.

Again in 1960, the police chief visited all the restaurant owners, telling each of them that all the waiters in Provincetown would have to get identity cards from the police if they wanted to work. The reason?

Ciro & Sal's baseball team, 1962 winners over Sal's Place in the Spaghetti League (l. to r., Fred Tasch, Victor Joren, Peter Hatch, Varujan Boghosian, Ciro, Dick Merkin, Paul Horowitz).

Ciro & Sal regulars, 1960 (l. to r., front row, Ester Bloom, Ciro, Harriot Miller; back row, Sunny Tascha, Barbara Kates, Grace Rizk, Romanos Rizk, Litsa Papoulias, Julian Deminski, Victor DeCarlo, Mihran Chobanian, Fred Tasch).

The town didn't like the image of too many homosexuals working as waiters. Everyone was fingerprinted and photographed. These records then circulated throughout the country, and if someone had been arrested for homosexuality (a felony in most states then), he was not allowed to work as a waiter.

Ciro was forced to relieve one waiter of his pad and pencil, but he refused to fire him; instead, he had him work in the kitchen for the next two years. When the law was finally changed, the young man returned to waiting tables. He has been with the restaurant ever since. Others were not so lucky, and a total of seventeen waiters lost their jobs that year. There was a movement for legal action over the constitutionality of this practice, but because none of the victims wanted to make a test case, nothing came of it.

In an effort to get everyone's mind off the problems, Ciro organized The Spaghetti League, a softball league made up of teams from all the restaurants in town. The games soon became a regular event, and every summer there was a showdown between Ciro and his crew, and Sal and his crew. The winning team got the Buitoni Award, a trophy designed to resemble a box of Buitoni spaghetti. The losing team had to host the winners for drinks. The league continued on into the 1970s when Ciro's team became known as "Ciro's 86ers" (by then the restaurant was known as CIRO'S).

If the sixties were a time of change, they were also a time of expansion for the restaurant. In 1962, Ciro purchased the building next door to the restaurant and built a kitchen five times the size of the original kitchen, which had been the size of a closet. With a larger kitchen, he was able to serve more people, but that meant he needed more space in which to seat them. A year later he solved this problem when he moved into a small house across the alley from the restaurant and began to convert his previous home above the restaurant into additional dining areas. The first year he converted only one room. Then in 1966 he added the second dining room, and in 1969 he finished the large, elegant bar. He did much of the design and construction himself.

All this time, Ciro continued to expand the restaurant menu. Each winter, while the restaurant was closed (it would not open during the winter until the 1980s), he would try different dishes at home and serve them to friends. The best and most practical ones would appear on the menu the following summer.

THE SEVENTIES

As the years went by and Ciro's success grew, he purchased many of the houses on Kiley Court. (In fact, it was often referred to as "Ciro's Alley.") He converted the house fronting the restaurant on Commercial Street into a gourmet specialty shop called "La Dispensa Di Ciro," and his wife, Patti, managed it. A young man from Baltimore worked there as a salesperson in the summer of 1971. He did not return the next summer, because John Waters's 1971 film, *Pink Flamingos*, made him into the camp star Divine.

The shop was later turned into a health food store. In 1984 it again became "La Dispensa Di Ciro," this time selling Italian specialty items and items from CIRO & SAL'S menu.

MENU, 1970s

Antipasto

ANTIPASTO—Salami, provolone, prosciutto, capacolla, olives, pimiento,
    anchovies, artichoke hearts, tomato and pickled vegetables 4.50
PROSCIUTTO CON MELONE—Italian ham with slices of cantaloupe. 4.50
CUORI DI CARCIOFI SOTT 'OLIO—Artichoke hearts in olive oil. 3.75
ACCIUGHE CON BURRO E LIMONE—Anchovies with butter and lemon . 2.25
CAPONATA—Sicilian diced eggplant and capers 2.75
CELERY AND OLIVES. 2.75
MELONE FRESCO—Melon in season. . . . . Quarter 2.00—Half 2.75
INSALATA DI SCAMPI—Shrimp Cocktail with lemon sauce or red sauce . . . 6.75
ARINGA MARINATA—Marinated Herring. 2.75
FUNGHI MARGHERITA—Marinated Mushrooms 3.25
CARPACCIO—Cold roast beef with capers and anchovy dressing 4.00
PÂTÉ 4.75
LITTLENECK CLAMS—on the half-shell 4.25
OYSTERS—on the half-shell 4.50
OYSTERS GIANNINI—oysters on the half-shell broiled with a pesto dressing. 5.00
PIATTO MISTO—Assorted shellfish and fish with dressing 6.25

Pasta

—Salad, bread and butter included with following dishes—All pasta cooked to order—
SPAGHETTI CON SALSA—Spaghetti with sauce. 7.50
SPAGHETTI CON POLPETTE—Spaghetti with meatballs 8.00
SPAGHETTI CON SALSICCIA—Spaghetti with Italian sausage. 8.00
SPAGHETTI CON PEPERONI—Spaghetti with roasted green peppers and
    sauce 8.00
SPAGHETTI CON FEGATINI DI POLLO—Spaghetti with chicken livers . . 9.00
SPAGHETTI AL PESTO—Genoa style pasta with a thick, pungent sauce of
    butter, sweet basil, garlic and parsley. 8.50
SPAGHETTI AL BURRO E FORMAGGIO—with a sauce of butter, romano
    cheese, garlic and parsley 8.00
SPAGHETTI CON AGLIO, OLIO E LIMONE—Spaghetti with garlic, olive
    oil and lemon 7.50
SPAGHETTI CON FUNGHI—Spaghetti with sauce and mushrooms sautéed
    in butter and prepared in wine. 8.00
SPAGHETTI ALLA MARINARA—Spaghetti with a sauce of Italian plum
    tomatoes, olive oil, garlic, and herbs. 7.50
SPAGHETTI ALLA PUTTENESCA—A very old Italian recipe. Sauce is
    prepared Quickly, with anchovies, tomatoes, black olives, chile peppers,
    herbs and spices. Nice fresh flavour. 8.00
SPAGHETTI ALLA FORIANA—A Lenten dish prepared in the village of
    Forio on the island of Ischia. Spaghetti with walnuts, anchovies, raisins,
    olive oil, garlic, herbs and pine nuts 9.75
SPAGHETTI CARBONARA—A specialty of Rome—Spaghetti with eggs,
    cheese and bits of lean bacon. 9.75
FETTUCCINE ALLA ROMANO—Ribbon like noodles, with butter,
    parmesan cheese, nutmeg and sweet cream. 10.25
Spaghetti substitutions 75¢ additional

Carne, Pesce

Pasta, Salad, bread and butter included with following dishes—

VITELLO ALLA MILANESE—Veal cutlet, breaded, served with butter and
lemon with spaghetti al burro e formaggio 13.00

VITELLO ALLA PARMIGIANA—Veal cutlet, breaded and baked with
tomato sauce, mozzarella and parmesan cheese........................ 13.00

VITELLO PICCATO—Thin slices of Veal sautéed in butter with dry white
wine, sliced fresh mushrooms, herbs, cream and lemon................ 14.75

VITELLO SCALOPPINE ALLA MARSALA—Wafers of veal marinated in
Marsala wine and cooked with Marsala, mushrooms, lemon and butter 14.75

NOCCE DI VITELLO BOLOGNESE—Thin slices of veal, prosciutto and
chicken livers prepared with a sauce of wine, soft cheese and herbs 14.75

VITELLO PHILOMENA—Veal with eggplant—Cubed veal, prepared with
eggplant, cheese, plum tomatoes, espagnole sauce and herbs—a Sicilian
delicacy 14.25

BISTECCA PIEMONTESE AL FERRI—Thick steak, broiled to order with
red wine and mushrooms............... New York Cut   —Tenderloin 17.95

SOGLIOLA SEMPLICE—Fillet of flounder is sautéed in oil with assorted
herbs, mushrooms, shallots, spices and Dry Vermouth................. 10.25

SOGLIOLA DI NOZZE—Sole—Poached in dry white wine—with a sauce
Amedeo... 10.50

STRIPED BASS ALLA PROCIDANA—Thick native striped bass steak
broiled with mint, wine vinegar, olive oil, and herbs................. 13.00

PESCE ALLA GIOSUE—Creation of Giosue from Rapallo—Fresh fish and
cherrystone clams with shallots—poached in white wine. 13.00

PESCE AZURO IN UMIDO—Neapolitan style, native fish prepared with
anchovies, olives, capers, plum tomatoes, herbs and red wine........... 10.50

COZZE ALLA COZZI—Mussels steamed in olive oil, garlic, white wine and
parsley 9.00

ZUPPA DI VONGOLE—Littleneck clams in the shell cooked in a pungent
seafood broth of tomato, herbs and wines.......................... 11.00

Piatto del Giorno

Sunday   —**LASAGNA AL FORNO**—Very wide strips of pasta baked in
layers with Italian sausage, small meatballs, hard-boiled eggs,
ragout sauce, parmesan cheese, mozzarella, ricotta 9.50

POLLO BERGAMO—Breast of Chicken with a filling of
almonds, mushrooms, fennel and sausage, with a sauce
Bechemel 11.00

PESCE MISTO IN BARCHETTA—salsa murano—Soft-
shelled crab, mussels, littlenecks, shrimp and fish with a
blended sauce of shallots, fennel, butter and pernod—en
casserole 14.75

Monday   —**MANICOTTI**—A thin, especially made pasta, rolled and
stuffed with prosciutto, ricotta, black olives, nuts, eggs, parsley,
romano cheese and mozzarella, and baked in tomato sauce..... 9.50

POLLO IN PADELLA—A delicacy of Possilipo—breast of
chicken prepared with a vegetable and herb stuffing and a light
wine sauce 11.00

VITELLO ALLA SFORZA—A saddle of veal cut into thick
chop—Broiled with a sauce espagnole and a touch of lemon ... 14.50

Tuesday —**ARROSTO DI ANGNELLO**—Thick slice of lamb from leg. Marinated in sherry, lemon juice and fresh rosemary and garlic and grilled to order. Served with hearts of artichoke, fried with cheese breading 13.50

POLLO BOLOGNESE—Half Chicken cut into pieces, cooked en casserole with herbs, cognac, puréed vegetables, sliced mushrooms and heavy cream 10.75

LASAGNA ALLA VENEZIA—Green lasagna noodles, with layers of broccoli, mushrooms, zucchini, with alternate layers of chicken, veal, pork, and ricotta. The sauces are besciamel and espagnole 11.25

Wednesday —**CANNELLONI VERDI**—A green, thinly-rolled pasta stuffed with pork, chicken, spinach, veal, and ricotta—served with a glazed cream sauce. 9.75

PETTI DI POLLO GENOVESE—Breast of chicken, artichoke hearts, egg plant, celery, and fresh mushrooms— seasoned with nutmeg, sage, garlic and wine—served en casserole. 11.00

CACCIUCCO LIVORNESE—Lobster, chicken, cherrystone clams, mussels and other varieties of seafood, baked in a light sauce of tomato, wine and herbs. 19.95

Thursday —**SALTIMBOCCA ALLA ROMANA**—Rolled thin veal cutlets stuffed with prosciutto, fresh savory herbs, garlic, sautéed in butter and chablis—served with lemon 14.75

MANICOTTI VERDI CON SPINACI E POLLO—A green pasta rolled and stuffed with ricotta, chicken and spinach 9.75

PETTI DI POLLO CON BROCCOLI—Breast of chicken (Supreme) with a prosciutto and mushroom filling, served on a bed of fresh broccoli, with a natural sauce 10.75

Friday —**SPAGHETTI CON VONGOLE IN BIANCO**—Spaghetti with clams, clam broth, olive oil, garlic, parsley, and pepper . . . 9.50

BRODETTO DI PESCE—Native fish with Littleneck Clams—cooked in a light sauce of plum tomatoes, wine, shallots and herbs 11.25

GIMINGNANO—Scallops broiled with a Madeira sauce and fresh mushrooms and lemon 14.95

POLLO ARRABBIATO—Half chicken baked in a spicy brown sauce with artichoke hearts, mancini peppers, and mushrooms 10.50

LASAGNA VERDI—Wide strips of spinach pasta baked in layers of ricotta, parmesan, romano, and mozzarella cheeses, eggs, spinach and a besciamel. 10.75

Saturday —**CANNELLONI**—A thinly rolled pasta stuffed with veal, chicken, beef and ricotta with a light tomato ragout. 9.75

SCAMPI ALLA GRIGLIA—Shrimp broiled in a sauce of butter, leeks, shallots, garlic, herbs and lemon 13.25

POLLO RAVINELLA—Half chicken, prepared with a sauce espagnole (piquante), baby onions, carrots and fresh mushrooms 10.50

OSSO BUCCO—Veal shank, braised with vegetables—con Risotto alla Milanese. 11.25

Specialita—other dishes which may be available

FEGATINI DI POLLO—Sautéed chicken livers in white wine and butter 9.25
with fresh mushrooms 9.50
FEGATINI DI POLLO ALLA SALVIA—Chicken livers with prosciutto,
marsala and savory 9.75
POLLO CASIMELLO—Sliced breast of chicken cooked in butter, herbs and
Madeira with prosciutto, and a soft mild cheese....................... 10.75
SOGLIOLA PRIMAVERA—Fillet of flounder sautéed in butter with a puréed
sauce of fresh herbs and vegetables 10.50
PESCE SARDENESE—From Sardinia, blue, haddock or cod, baked with
chopped fresh tomato, green pepper, scallions, fresh lime and coriander ... 11.00
MOLECHE DI SAN GENNARO—Sautéed soft-shelled crabs with shallots,
herbs and dry white wine, served on a bed of zucchini.................. 11.75
MEDALLIONE DI VITELLO—Veal tenderloin cut in medallions, sautéed in
butter and brandy, served with mushrooms........................... 16.50
FETTUCINE AL ANDREA—with sweet cream, parmesan, mushrooms, and
slices of zucchini... 10.75
PASTA ABBUZZESSE—Pasta with seafood sauce—mussels, shrimp, clams,
scallops and squid.. 11.75
INVOLTINI DI BUE—Slices of Rib-eye, rolled, with a filling of prosciutto,
eggplant, cheese, and herbs. Served with Eggplant Andulese 11.75

These dishes are not prepared every day. Please refer to Piatto del Giorno or ask waiter for availability.
Salad, bread and butter included with the above dishes.

THE EIGHTIES

By 1980 Ciro had purchased another Provincetown restaurant just one block from CIRO & SAL'S. Christened "The Flagship Restaurant," it extends out over the bay and offers American nouvelle cuisine.

In addition, he opened a CIRO & SAL'S in Boston which serves the same fine Italian food found in the Provincetown restaurant. He continues to experiment, refining old recipes and developing new ones. He has also successfully packaged and frozen many of the menu items from CIRO & SAL'S. Still more plans are on the drawing board.

An artist himself, Ciro has been deeply involved in Provincetown's art community, which he considers an essential part of not only his own life but also that of the town. For over twenty years he has been a member of the Provincetown Art Association and Museum, and he served as its president for eight years. (He is now president emeritus.) In recent years, Ciro and his wife Patti have hosted an annual garden party where residents gather to enjoy good food and show their support for the museum. It has now become yet another Provincetown tradition and is a highlight of each summer season.

The 1980s have also seen a constant stream of young aspiring chefs and Ciro's relatives passing through the various restaurants, working in every aspect of the business. Some have stayed on; others have gone on to open their own successful restaurants. Ciro's oldest daughter manages the Provincetown restaurants, and his youngest, a graduate of the New York Restaurant School, has been both cook and manager for each of the restaurants and assists her father with his many projects.

Now there is another generation—Ciro's two grandchildren—growing up in the restaurant. And another generation has joined the staff as well. A tradition happily continues. . . .

Ciro, early '80's.

The "crew," early '80's.

Al DiLauro and Betty Alexander, '80's.

PART

II

THE
RECIPES

ANTIPASTI

Appetizers

I first got to know Ciro in the spring of 1956. We were both working on the Air Force base in North Truro, Ciro as a carpenter and I as a laborer. Today, probably few people think of Ciro as a carpenter, but he was a fine craftsman (he had also worked at Flyer's Boatyard), and I acknowledge with gratitude the skills I learned from him.

In the restaurant's early years, Ciro had to do the carpentry work to supplement his income during the winter, when the restaurant was closed. Later, when he became more successful, Ciro designed and built additions onto the small, original cellar room, and construction usually went on until the last minute, as it did the time Ciro put the floor in in the back room the morning the restaurant opened. Ralph Santos, the great P-town mason, poured the floor and placed the flagstones in place, hoping that everything would set before the opening just a few hours away. Perhaps to divert the guests' attention away from their precarious footing, Ciro made the punch super-strong that night. Before long, everyone was floating euphorically over a floor that was still wet in places.

A year or two later Ciro, Eldred Mowery and I were putting up the main timbers of the upstairs dining room. The finale was the placement of the roof beam, a massive trunk that weighed over two hundred pounds. We manhandled the monster into place, secured it and went on to other things. Days later, we took down the scaffolding under the great beam and to our horror found that all that secured it was one six-penny nail.

For me, these episodes are the essence of Ciro—sometimes shaky underfoot, but always reaching for the sky, no matter what. Keep on, Ciro. Bravo!

TONY VEVERS

◆————————◆

Any of the salads and pasta salads can be used as appetizers or as part of an "antipasto composto." This would be a platter filled with a variety of foods. Here are some suggestions:

Sliced cured meats

Sliced cheeses

Cold, blanched vegetables dressed in extra virgin olive oil

Giardiniera (see recipe)

Supplì (see recipe)

Frittura composta (see recipe)

Frittata or frittata di pasta (see recipe), cut in wedges

Olives

Anchovies or sardines or tuna

Shellfish, poached and served dressed in olive oil and vinegar or herbed aioli.

Piatto misto (see recipe)

Aringa marinata (see recipe)

Ostriche al Giannini (see recipe)

◆————————◆

FRITTURA COMPOSTA
Mixed Platter of Fried Foods

This is a platter of various meats, fish, vegetables and cheeses that have been cut into bite-size pieces, dipped in egg and flour, and fried in olive oil. The various foods are then arranged on a large platter and garnished with lemon wedges.

The frittura is usually served as a meal, but it may also be used as an appetizer or as part of an *antipasto composto*. How you compose the frittura is up to you. Try to get a variety of tastes and textures, although you can do a frittura composed entirely of fish or vegetables, if you so desire. Here are some possible ingredients:

Veal fillets (pounded and cut into thin strips)
Sweetbreads (cleaned and blanched*)
Brains (cleaned and blanched*)
Fish (if tiny, leave whole; if large, fillet and cut into thin strips)
Shrimp (whole)
Squid (cut into thick rings)
Artichoke hearts (cut in quarters)
Cauliflower flowerets (blanched)
Zucchini (cut into sticks)
Zucchini blossoms (whole with stamen removed)
Beets (sliced in thin circles)
Supplì (see recipe)
Mozzarella in Carozza (see recipe)

*To prepare the sweetbreads, soak them for ½ hour in cold water. Remove them from the water and place them in a casserole pan. Cover the sweetbreads with water and bring to a boil. Remove the pan from the heat and let the sweetbreads cool in their cooking water. Once cooled, remove them from the water, remove any excess membranes and cut them into 2-inch pieces. Pat dry.

*To prepare the brains, soak them as you would the sweetbreads. Place them in a casserole pan, cover them with cold water and add a pinch of salt and about a tablespoon of white vinegar. Bring the water to a boil, and just as soon as it boils, remove the brains and place in cold water to cool completely. Once cooled, remove them from the water and cut them into 1-inch pieces. Pat dry.

The various foods can be prepared for frying in three ways. First, they can be dipped in a pastella, or batter. To make the pastella, mix ½ cup flour with one cup water (it should be thick). Add a pinch of salt and 2 teaspoons olive oil. Just before you are ready to use the pastella, fold in 2 softly beaten egg whites. Dip in the pieces of food and fry. This works well with vegetables.

Second, simply dip the foods in flour seasoned with salt and pepper, and then dip them in beaten eggs also seasoned with salt and pepper. This works well with fishes and meats. If frying fish, try adding a little cornmeal to the flour.

Third, same as for the second method, but after dipping them in the egg, dip them in finely grated dry bread crumbs. This works well with cheeses and meats.

Fry the foods separately and try to keep the oil at the appropriate temperature. Medium heat works well with foods that have a high water content, like potatoes. Medium heat also works best for thick fish and meat. Higher heat is used for foods that are already partially or entirely cooked. Very high heat is used for small items that will cook quickly.

Drain the foods on paper towels or brown paper and keep in a warm (250 degree) oven until you have finished making the frittura.

Arrange all the foods on a platter. Garnish with sliced fresh lemon and chopped parsley. Serve immediately.

GIARDINIERA
Marinated Vegetables

Cut an assortment of vegetables in bite-size cubes, circles and flowerets. The giardiniera should be colorful, so choose your vegetables accordingly (cauliflower, carrots, broccoli, beets, celery, sweet red peppers, zucchini, etc.). Blanche and shock the vegetables separately. (See Glossary for cooking technique.) Pat them dry.

Layer the vegetables in a glass jar and cover them with white wine vinegar. Seal the jar and let the vegetables marinate for at least 24 hours.

The giardiniera can be served as is, or it can be tossed with extra virgin olive oil, Maionese or Aioli, and seasoned further with fresh herbs, salt and pepper. Serve as part of an antipasto.

CUORI DI CARCIOFI SOTT 'OLIO

Artichoke Hearts in Olive Oil

SERVES 4

12   *fresh artichokes*
    Juice of 1 lemon
    Salt
¼   *cup extra virgin olive oil*
1   *tablespoon fresh lemon juice*
1   *garlic clove, pressed*
1   *teaspoon dried basil or chopped fresh basil leaves*
    Salt and freshly ground black pepper
4   *lemon wedges or slices*

Remove all the leaves and the chokes from the artichokes. Cook the artichoke hearts in simmering water, with the lemon juice and salt to taste until they are tender. They should still be firm (*al dente*). Drain and cool.

In a bowl, mix together all the remaining ingredients except the lemon wedges. Add the artichoke hearts and toss to mix thoroughly. Marinate at room temperature for 3 hours before serving with the lemon wedges.

ASPARAGI CON PROSCIUTTO

Asparagus with Prosciutto

SERVES 4

24   *thin asparagus spears*
8   *thin slices prosciutto, trimmed of excess fat*

Break or cut off the tough parts of the asparagus stems so that all of the spears are of equal length. Steam the asparagus until they are tender but firm (*al dente*). Plunge the cooked spears into ice water to stop the cooking, then drain and dry thoroughly.

Gather 3 spears together in a bundle and wrap a slice of prosciutto around the spears. Make 7 additional bundles in the same way.

Lightly dress each bundle with extra virgin olive oil or Pesto (page 89) to which extra olive oil has been added.

CAPONATA
Marinated Eggplant

SERVES 8

2   medium-size eggplants, cut into ¾-inch cubes
     Salt
¾   cup olive oil
1   cup celery cut into large dice
2   medium-size onions, cut into large dice
1   1-pound, 12-ounce can imported Italian plum tomatoes,
          strained, seeded and chopped
¼   cup capers, rinsed and drained
½   cup pitted green olives, cut in half
3   tablespoons red wine vinegar
1   teaspoon sugar
     Salt and freshly ground black pepper

Put the eggplant cubes into a colander and sprinkle them with salt. Weight them down with a plate and let drain for 30 minutes. Rinse the eggplant in cool running water and dry it well.

Heat the oil in a saucepan and cook the eggplant until it is lightly browned. Remove the eggplant with a slotted spoon, leaving the oil in the pan.

Add the onions and celery to the pan and cook until the onions are translucent. Add the tomatoes and cook for 12 minutes.

Add the eggplant, capers, olives, vinegar, sugar and salt and pepper to taste. Cook over low heat for 8 minutes. Serve hot or at room temperature.

FUNGHI SOTT' OLIO E ACETO
Marinated Mushrooms

SERVES 4 TO 6

1   pound fresh mushrooms
2   garlic cloves, pressed
¼   teaspoon ground turmeric

½   cup extra virgin olive oil
¼   cup fresh lemon juice
2   tablespoons red wine vinegar
     Salt and freshly ground pepper

Cut the ends from the stems of the mushrooms. Wash or wipe the mushrooms thoroughly; then cut them into thick slices.

Mix together all the remaining ingredients in a bowl and add the mushrooms. Toss to mix well, being careful not to break the mushrooms. Marinate at room temperature for at least 3 hours before serving.

MOZZARELLA IN CAROZZA
Mozzarella in a Carriage

SERVES 4

4   large eggs, beaten
½   cup heavy cream
     Salt and freshly ground black pepper
12   ¾-inch-thick slices fresh mozzarella
1   cup fine bread crumbs, toasted
2   cups vegetable oil

Mix together the eggs and cream. Season with salt and pepper. Dip the slices of mozzarella into the egg wash and let the excess drip off.

Season the bread crumbs with salt and pepper. Pat the mozzarella slices into the crumbs to coat them thoroughly.

Heat the oil to 350 degrees in a heavy skillet. Fry the mozzarella for 1 minute on each side, or until golden brown. Drain briefly on paper towels and serve immediately.

MOZZARELLA IN CAROZZA CON ACCIUGHE
Mozzarella in a Carriage with Anchovies

SERVES 2 TO 4

8   ¼-inch-thick slices Italian bread
4   ¼-inch-thick slices fresh mozzarella
4   anchovy fillets, rinsed, dried and coarsely chopped
¼   cup all-purpose flour
2   large eggs
     Pinch of salt
¼   cup olive oil

Remove the crusts from the bread and cut each slice in half on the diagonal to create two triangles. Ideally, the triangles should be about 2 inches long and 1 inch wide at the base.

Cut the slices of mozzarella to fit the bread triangles. Place each slice of mozzarella on a slice of bread. Add a little of the chopped anchovies. Cover with another slice of bread to create a sandwich.

Dip only the edges of the sandwiches in the flour. This will keep the mozzarella from oozing out when it is cooked.

Now place a small amount of tepid water in a low, flat pan and moisten the floured edges of the sandwich in the water. Set the sandwiches on a plate. They should not touch.

Beat the eggs and salt in a shallow pan large enough to hold all the sandwiches. Arrange all the sandwiches in the pan and allow them to absorb the eggs for 15 to 20 minutes on each side. All the egg should be absorbed.

Heat the oil in a skillet and fry the sandwiches until they are golden brown on both sides. Drain briefly on paper towels and serve immediately.

BRUSCHETTE

Toasted Bread with Olive Oil

These are perfect for a light meal or as hors d'oeuvres.

The basic technique is very simple. Take a thick slice of Italian bread. Rub both sides of the bread with a slice of garlic. (This can also be done after the bread has been toasted.) Sprinkle a generous amount of extra virgin olive oil on both sides. Toast the bread in the oven, broil it or grill it on both sides until it is crispy on the outside but still soft on the inside. Be careful not to burn it.

The bruschette may be eaten as is or with a variety of toppings. Here are some suggestions:

Fresh mozzarella, tomatoes and basil
Tomato slices and salt
A purée of cannellini beans and tuna
Fagioli al Fiasco (see recipe)
Sliced Italian cured meats (especially prosciutto)

SUPPLÌ

Filled Rice Balls

SERVES 6

12   ounces *(about 2 cups) Arborio rice*
1   *cup Sugo di Pomodoro Semplice (page 85)*
1½ *cups water*
2   *tablespoons butter*
2   *ounces grated Parmigiano*
2   *large eggs, beaten*

FILLINGS

    Mozzarella, cut into small cubes
    Chopped prosciutto
    Sautéed chopped onions
    Chopped fresh herbs
    Sautéed chopped fresh mushrooms
    Pre-soaked chopped porcini mushrooms
    Pecorino or caciotta, chopped
1   *cup fine dry breadcrumbs*
2   *cups olive oil or lard*

Put the rice, tomato sauce and water in a saucepan. Cover the pan and bring to a boil. Lower the heat and simmer the rice until it is tender. There should be no excess liquid.

Remove the pan from the heat and stir in the butter, grated cheese and eggs. Fresh herbs may be added at this point. Turn the mixture out onto a plate. Spread it over the plate and let it cool completely.

Prepare the filling of your choice.

Put a rounded tablespoon of rice into the palm of your hand. Make a well in the center and add a little bit of the filling. Squeeze the rice over and around the filling to form a compact ball. Roll the ball in the bread crumbs, covering it entirely. Put the completed rice ball on a baking sheet. Continue making rice balls in this way until all the rice has been used. Be sure that the rice balls do not touch on the baking sheet.

Heat the oil or lard in a large pan with low sides, being careful not to let the oil get so hot that it smokes. Fry the rice balls in the oil until they are golden all over. Drain them on brown paper or paper towels and serve immediately.

The supplì can be served as an hors d'oeuvre, an appetizer, a snack or as part of a frittura composta.

PROSCIUTTO CON MELONE
Prosciutto with Melon

SERVES 4

1   *ripe cantaloupe or honeydew melon*
½   *pound prosciutto, thinly sliced and trimmed of excess fat*
4   *lemon wedges or slices*

Cut the melon in half from top to bottom. Remove the seeds and membranes. Then cut the melon into 1-inch-thick slices and remove the rind.

Arrange the wedges on a serving plate. Lay the slices of prosciutto across the wedges of fruit, or wrap the prosciutto around the wedges. Serve with lemon wedges.

CARPACCIO
Raw Beef with Capers

SERVES 6

1	pound raw, lean, beef fillet
½	cup extra virgin olive oil
¼	cup fresh lemon juice
¼	cup plus 2 tablespoons capers, rinsed and drained
6	anchovy fillets, rinsed and drained
1	teaspoon Dijon mustard
2	garlic cloves, finely chopped
¼	teaspoon freshly ground black pepper

Trim the beef of all the outside fat.

Slice the meat very thinly. An electric slicer works best for this. It is essential that the meat be sliced as thinly as possible.

Put the oil, lemon juice, ¼ cup of the capers, anchovy fillets, Dijon mustard, garlic and black pepper in a food processor or blender and process until smooth.

Arrange the slices of meat, overlapping, on a flat serving plate. The plate should be completely covered. Garnish the meat with the remaining 2 tablespoons of capers. Serve the sauce on the side.

PÂTÉ DI CAMPAGNA
Country Pâté

SERVES 8 TO 10

2	pounds fatty pork, ground
2	pounds fatty veal, ground
1	pound pork livers or calf's liver, ground
1	cup cooked ham or tongue, diced
1½	cups finely chopped onion
6	garlic cloves, finely chopped
1	teaspoon dried thyme
1	teaspoon ground allspice

2   *tablespoons salt*
1½   *teaspoons freshly ground white pepper*
¾   *cup cognac*
1½   *pounds fresh pork fat, thinly sliced*
5   *bay leaves*
1   *tablespoon chopped fresh rosemary leaves*

Combine all the ingredients, except the pork fat, bay leaves and rosemary, in a ceramic or enamel bowl. Mix thoroughly, cover, and refrigerate overnight.

The next day preheat the oven to 350 degrees. Line the bottom and sides of a 5- by 9- by 3-inch loaf pan with the pork fat. Allow the fat to hang over the sides by about 2 inches. Press the meat mixture firmly into the loaf pan. Bang the pan on the table a couple of times to make sure the meat is firmly settled in the pan. Fold the pork fat over the meat to cover it. Lay the bay leaves in a single row down the center and sprinkle the rosemary over the entire surface.

Cover the pan tightly with a double thickness of aluminum foil. Place the pâté pan into a slightly larger pan and fill this pan with enough warm water to reach halfway up the sides of the pâté pan. Bake the pâté for 1½ hours.

When the pâté has finished cooking, remove it from the pan with the water and let it cool at room temperature for 1 hour. Next, place a pan that is slightly smaller than the pâté mold on top of the pâté. Fill the pan with heavy objects. Refrigerate the weighted down pâté overnight.

The next day remove the weights and the foil from the pâté. Dip the pan in hot water and turn the pâté out onto a plate. Serve immediately or cover tightly and keep refrigerated until you are ready to use it. (The pâté will keep for a week.)

PIATTO MISTO
Marinated Shellfish

SERVES 4 TO 6

½   pound unshelled medium-size shrimp
½   pound sea scallops
1½   dozen mussels, scrubbed and debearded
4   tablespoons red wine vinegar
½   cup extra virgin olive oil
¼   cup fresh lemon juice
2   garlic cloves, pressed
¼   teaspoon dried marjoram
     Salt and freshly ground black pepper

Bring 3 quarts of water to a boil and add a tablespoon of the vinegar. Add the shrimp and scallops and return the water to a boil. Cook the shellfish for 2 minutes, then drain and rinse in cold water.

Put the mussels in a saucepan with ¼ inch of water. Cover the pan and cook over medium heat until the shells open. Remove them from the pan and let cool. Remove the mussels from the shells.

Shell and devein the shrimp.

Combine the shellfish in a bowl. Blend together the remaining ingredients and pour the dressing over the shellfish. Toss well to mix. Cover and refrigerate for 2 hours before serving.

INSALATA DI SCAMPI
Shrimp Salad

SERVES 4

1   pound unshelled medium-size shrimp
½   cup extra virgin olive oil
¼   cup fresh lemon juice
1   garlic clove, pressed
     Salt and freshly ground black pepper

Bring 2 quarts of water to a boil. Drop in the shrimp and continue to simmer for 2 to 3 minutes. Drain the shrimp and let them cool. Shell and devein the shrimp and refrigerate until ready to use.

Mix together the remaining ingredients.

Arrange the shrimp on a cold serving plate and pour some of the dressing over them, or serve it separately as a dipping sauce.

OSTRICHE AL GIANNINI

Broiled Oysters

SERVES 2 TO 6

24   fresh oysters (Wellfleet oysters if you can find them)
½   cup Pesto (page 89)
½   cup fresh grated Parmigiano
1   cup fresh bread crumbs
2   tablespoons olive oil

Preheat the oven to 450 degrees.

Rinse and open the oysters, leaving them on the half shell and being careful to keep their juices in the shell.

Place the oysters on a baking sheet. Balance them on each other if necessary to keep the juices from spilling out.

Top each oyster with ½ teaspoon of Pesto and a sprinkle of Parmigiano. Mix the bread crumbs with the oil. Place 1 teaspoon of the bread crumb mixture on each oyster.

Bake or broil the oysters until the crumbs are golden brown.

CALAMARI PICCANTI

Squid with Anchovies and Lemon

SERVES 4

12   squid, cleaned
8   tablespoons butter
8   anchovy fillets, rinsed and dried
4   tablespoons dry white wine
1   cup heavy cream
4   teaspoons fresh lemon juice
     Salt and freshly ground black pepper
4   lemon slices

Slice the squid into ¼-inch-thick rings. Leave the tentacles whole.

Melt the butter in a skillet. Add the anchovy fillets to the butter and mash them with a fork to dissolve them. Add the squid to the pan. Raise the heat to moderate and sauté for 5 minutes. Add the wine and let it reduce for a moment. Add the cream, raise the heat and reduce the sauce for 1 minute.

Remove the squid to a warm serving dish.

Add the lemon juice and salt and pepper to taste to the sauce and continue to reduce it until it is slightly thickened.

Pour the sauce over the squid and serve garnished with the lemon slices.

ARINGA MARINATA

Marinated Herring

Pommerey mustard
Maionese (see recipe)
Lemon juice
Pinch of cayenne pepper
Pickled herring, cut into ¼-inch-thick slices
Romaine or Boston Lettuce
Lemon slices

Mix 2 parts mustard and one part maionese. Add a squeeze of lemon juice and a pinch of cayenne pepper and mix well.

Add the herring to the sauce and toss well.

Serve the herring on a bed of lettuce. Garnish with lemon slices.

One portion would be one whole herring fillet.

SALMONE AFFUMICATO

Smoked Salmon

Smoked salmon
Romaine or Boston lettuce
Horseradish
Heavy cream
Freshly ground black pepper
Whole capers, rinsed
Bermuda onion, sliced into thin rounds

Slice the smoked salmon on the bias in ⅛-inch-thick slices.

Line a dish with romaine or Boston lettuce. Arrange the slices of salmon on the lettuce.

Beat together the heavy cream and horseradish to make a thick sauce. Season with freshly ground black pepper. Pour a little of this sauce over the salmon slices.

Sprinkle whole capers over the salmon. Finally, arrange thin slices of Bermuda onion over the salmon.

One portion would be 3 to 4 ounces of salmon.

MINESTRE E BRODI

Soups and Stocks

One night a large group of people was having dinner at the restaurant. Varujan Boghosian came in and ordered champagne for everyone in the party. When they had finished eating, he ordered after-dinner drinks for them all. He assured Ciro that he needn't worry about the check. When the waitress presented him with the bill, he simply ate it!

◆———————◆

MINESTRONE CON FAGIOLI E SALSICCIA
Minestrone with Beans and Sausages

SERVES 6

1	cup dried cannellini beans or chickpeas, sorted and rinsed
¼	cup olive oil
4	Italian sweet sausages
4	garlic cloves, finely chopped
1	onion, chopped
2	carrots, cut into ¼-inch-thick slices
2	celery stalks, thickly cut on the diagonal
2	teaspoons dried thyme
1	bay leaf

1   teaspoon dried oregano
1   teaspoon chopped fresh rosemary leaves
½   teaspoon fennel seeds, crushed
½   cup dry red wine
5   cups veal stock (page 50)
2   small zucchini, cut into ½-inch pieces
1   sweet green pepper, cut into ½-inch pieces
½   pound plum tomatoes, peeled, seeded and coarsely chopped
2   tablespoons tomato paste
     Salt and freshly ground black pepper
¼   pound ditalini
½   cup Pesto (page 89), optional
     Freshly grated Parmigiano

Soak the beans overnight in water to cover. Drain them and cover with fresh water. Cover the pot and bring to a boil, then lower the heat and cook the beans for 45 minutes to 2 hours (the chickpeas will take the longer time to cook).

Heat the oil in a heavy saucepan. Add the whole sausages, and brown them on all sides. Remove the sausages and set them aside. Add the garlic, onion, carrot and celery to the pan. Sauté until the vegetables are tender. Add the herbs, wine and stock. Bring to a boil. Add the zucchini, green pepper, tomatoes, tomato paste and the cooked, drained beans. Slice the sausage into ¼-inch-thick rounds and add them to the soup. Simmer for 20 minutes.

While the soup is cooking, cook the ditalini in salted boiling water until it is very *al dente*. Drain the ditalini and add it to the soup. You may not have to add all the ditalini; it should not overpower the other ingredients. Season with salt and pepper to taste. Continue to cook the soup for 10 minutes more.

If desired, stir in the Pesto just before serving. Serve with freshly grated Parmigiano.

MINESTRA DI LENTICHIE
Lentil Soup

SERVES 6

¼   cup olive oil
2   ounces prosciutto, untrimmed and in 1 piece
1   onion, finely chopped
1   carrot, finely chopped
1   celery stalk, finely chopped
3   garlic cloves, finely chopped
3   cups lentils, sorted and rinsed
2   teaspoons dried thyme
1   teaspoon ground cumin
1   bay leaf
½   cup dry red wine
6   cups veal stock (page 50)
2   tomatoes, peeled, seeded and chopped
1   tablespoon dry mustard
1   tablespoon red wine vinegar
    Salt and freshly ground black pepper

Heat the olive oil in a large heavy saucepan. Add the proscuitto, onion, carrot, celery and garlic. Sauté, stirring occasionally, until the vegetables are soft.

Add the lentils, herbs, wine and stock. Cover the pot and bring to a boil. Lower the heat and cook slowly for 1 to 2 hours, or until the lentils are tender. If the lentils start to get dry, add more stock.

Add the remaining ingredients to the soup. Cook for 15 minutes longer. Serve immediately.

For a variation, ⅓ to ½ of the soup may be passed through a food-mill and then added back to the whole lentils. Garnish with a dollop of sour cream and extra chopped tomatoes.

MINESTRA DI ZUCCHINI CON POMODORI E BASILICO

Zucchini Soup with Tomatoes and Basil

SERVES 6

4   tablespoons butter
1   onion, finely chopped
1   small carrot, finely chopped
½   celery stalk, finely chopped
4   garlic cloves, finely chopped
4   medium-size zucchini, chopped
2   teaspoons dried thyme
1   bay leaf
½   cup dry white wine
4   cups chicken stock (page 51)
4   large ripe tomatoes, peeled, seeded and chopped
6   fresh basil leaves, chopped
     Salt and freshly ground black pepper
½   cup light cream, at room temperature
     Fresh basil leaves for garnish

Melt the butter in a heavy saucepan. Add the onion, carrot, celery and garlic and sauté the vegetables until they are tender.

Add the zucchini and herbs, stir, and sauté for 15 minutes.

Add the wine and stock to the pot and bring to a boil. Cover the pot and cook for 35 to 40 minutes.

Remove the soup from the heat and purée it in a food processor or blender. Pour the purée into the top of a double boiler over simmering water. Add the chopped tomatoes and basil. Season with salt and pepper to taste.

Pour a ladleful of the soup into the cream and then pour the mixture back into the soup. Heat slowly. Garnish each serving with fresh basil leaves.

MINESTRA DI FINOCCHIO
Fennel Soup

SERVES 6

4	tablespoons butter
1	leek, white part only, finely chopped
1	medium-size carrot, finely chopped
3	garlic cloves, finely chopped
1	teaspoon dried thyme
1	bay leaf
2	heads fresh fennel
½	cup dry white wine
4	cups chicken stock (page 51)
½ to ¾	cup light cream, at room temperature
	Salt and freshly ground black pepper
2	tablespoons anise-flavored liqueur, such as Anisette, Pernod, Sambuca, etc.

Melt the butter in a heavy saucepan. Add the leek, carrot and garlic, and sauté until the vegetables are tender. Add the thyme and bay leaf.

Remove the green parts and the stem from the fennel bulbs. (Reserve these to use in making vegetable broth (p. 52.) Coarsely chop the bulbs and add them to the pan. Sauté for 10 minutes.

Add the wine and chicken stock and bring to a boil. Lower the heat and simmer, covered, for 30 to 40 minutes.

Remove the soup from the heat and purée it in a blender or food processor. Pour the purée into the top of a double boiler over simmering water. Pour a ladleful of the soup into the cream, and then pour the mixture back into the soup. Season with salt and pepper to taste. Stir in the liqueur and heat slowly until hot.

MINESTRA DI CAVOLFIORE
Cauliflower Soup

Simply substitute one head of cauliflower, flowerets only, for the fennel.

CREMA DI FUNGHI CON ZAFFERANO
Mushroom Soup with Saffron

SERVES 6

4	tablespoons butter
1	onion, finely chopped
1	carrot, finely chopped
1	celery stalk, finely chopped
3	garlic cloves, finely chopped
1	pound fresh mushrooms, cleaned and sliced
2	teaspoons dried thyme
1	bay leaf
½	cup dry white wine
4	cups veal stock (page 50)
¼	cup cream sherry
2	pinches of saffron threads
½ to ¾	cup light cream, at room temperature
	Salt and freshly ground black pepper

Melt the butter in a heavy saucepan. Add the onion, carrot, celery and garlic and sauté until the vegetables are tender. Add the mushrooms, thyme and bay leaf, stir, and sauté for 10 minutes.

Add the wine and stock and bring to a boil. Cover the pan, lower the heat and cook for 30 to 40 minutes.

Remove the soup from the heat and purée it in a blender or food processor. Pour the purée into the top of a double boiler over simmering water. Add the sherry and saffron and cook for 10 minutes.

Pour a ladleful of the soup into the cream, and then pour the mixture back into the soup. Season with salt and pepper to taste.

NOTE: Dried porcini mushrooms that have been soaked, can be added to the soup for a more complex flavor.

PURÈ DI POMODORO CON PESTO
Purée of Tomato Soup with Pesto

SERVES 6

4	tablespoons butter
4	garlic cloves, finely chopped
1	onion, finely chopped
1	small carrot, finely chopped
1 to 1½	pounds ripe tomatoes, peeled, seeded and chopped
2	teaspoons dried thyme
1	bay leaf
1	teaspoon dried oregano
½	cup dry white wine
4	cups chicken stock (page 51)
½	cup light cream, at room temperature
½	cup Pesto (page 89)
	Salt and freshly ground black pepper

Melt the butter in a heavy saucepan. Add the garlic, onions and carrot, and sauté until the vegetables are tender. Add the tomatoes, thyme, bay leaf and oregano. Stir and cook for 5 minutes.

Add the wine and chicken stock and bring to a boil. Cover the pot, lower the heat and cook for 30 minutes.

Remove the soup from the heat and purée it in a blender or food processor. Pour the purée into the top of a double boiler over simmering water. Pour a ladleful of the soup into the cream, and then pour the mixture back into the soup. Swirl in the Pesto, and season the soup with salt and pepper to taste. Heat slowly.

NOTE: This soup may also be chilled and served as a cold summertime soup.

BRODO DI CARNE

Beef Stock

YIELD: 5 QUARTS

6 to 8	pounds beef bones, chopped
4	ounces (½ cup) lard or pork fat
2	pounds beef chuck or trimmings
1	medium-size onion, peeled and cut into quarters
1	large celery stalk, cut into quarters
1	medium-size carrot, peeled and cut into quarters
2	large cloves garlic, unpeeled
6 to 7	quarts cold water
½	cup tomato purée
1	cup dry red wine
½	teaspoon salt
1	bay leaf
¼	teaspoon crushed black peppercorns
½	bunch parsley sprigs (stems and leaves), washed

Preheat the oven to 400 degrees.

Rinse the bones in cold water and pat them dry with paper towels.

Put the lard in a roasting pan and melt it in the oven. Add the bones and beef and brown them lightly, stirring occasionally. Add the vegetables and brown them along with the beef bones.

Remove the pan from the oven and drain off the fat. Transfer the contents of the roasting pan to a large stock pot and add the cold water. Cover the pot and bring the water to a boil over high heat. Skim off any foam or fat and add the remaining ingredients. Bring the stock back to a boil and then lower the heat to keep the stock at a simmer. Let it cook for 3 hours. Skim the surface of the stock as necessary.

After 3 hours, strain the stock through a fine mesh strainer (see Note). Discard the bones, etc., and let the stock cool.

The stock can be stored tightly covered in the refrigerator for several days or it can be frozen in pint or quart containers and used as needed.

NOTE: If a clearer stock is desired, line the strainer with cheesecloth.

BRODO DI VITELLO

Veal Stock

YIELD: 5 QUARTS

5 to 6	pounds veal bones, cut up
6	quarts cold water
1	cup dry white wine
1	large onion, cut in half
2	celery stalks, cut in half
1	whole tomato, seeded
1	small carrot, peeled
½	bunch parsley sprigs (stems and leaves), washed
½	teaspoon dried thyme
1	bay leaf
½	teaspoon crushed black peppercorns

Rinse the bones in cold water.

Place the bones in a large stock pot and add the cold water (see Note). Cover the pot and bring the water to a boil. Skim off any foam or fat that rises to the surface.

Add the remaining ingredients and return the stock to a boil. Lower the heat and simmer the stock for 2 hours. Skim the surface of the stock as necessary.

Strain the stock through a fine mesh strainer and discard the bones, etc. Let the stock cool. Store in pint or quart containers in the refrigerator or freezer.

NOTE: Veal trimmings may be added to the stock for extra flavor.

BRODO DI POLLO

Chicken Stock

YIELD: 5 QUARTS

5 to 6   *pounds chicken bones, or 1 3-pound whole chicken*
6   *quarts cold water*
1   *cup dry white wine*
1   *large onion, peeled and cut in half*
1   *medium-size carrot, peeled and cut in half*
2   *celery stalks, cut in half*
1   *teaspoon dried thyme*
½   *bunch parsley sprigs (leaves and stems), washed*
1   *bay leaf*
¼   *teaspoon crushed black peppercorns*

Rinse the bones or chicken in cold water, put them in a large stock pot and add the cold water (see Note). Cover the pot and bring the water to a boil over high heat. Skim off any foam or fat that rises to the surface.

Add the remaining ingredients and return the stock to a boil. Lower the heat and simmer for 2 hours. Skim the surface as necessary.

Strain the stock through a fine mesh strainer and discard the bones, etc. Let the stock cool and store in pint or quart containers in the refrigerator or freezer.

NOTE: For a darker, richer stock, the bones and vegetables may be browned in 2 to 4 ounces (¼ to ½ cup) fat in a 400-degree oven before being added to the stock pot.

BRODO DI LEGUMI

Vegetable Stock

YIELD: 5 QUARTS

¼	cup olive oil
1	large onion, coarsely chopped
2	large celery stalks, coarsely chopped
2	fennel stalks, coarsely chopped
1	zucchini, coarsely chopped
1	garlic clove, unpeeled
6	quarts cold water
1	cup dry white wine
1	bay leaf
1	teaspoon dried thyme
1	small bunch parsley sprigs (stems and leaves), washed

Heat the oil in a large stock pot. Add the vegetables and sauté until they are golden. Add the remaining ingredients, cover, and bring to a boil. Lower the heat and simmer the stock for 1 hour.

Strain the stock through a fine mesh strainer and let cool. Store in pint or quart containers in the refrigerator or freezer.

BRODO DI PESCE

Fish Stock

YIELD: 5 QUARTS

5	pounds fish bones, heads and tails
5	quarts cold water
1	cup dry white wine
1	small onion, peeled
1	celery stalk
1	garlic clove, unpeeled
1	bay leaf
5	parsley sprigs (leaves and stems), washed
1	teaspoon salt

If you are using the heads from round fish (as opposed to flat fish, such as flounder), remove the gills and discard so that they will not release blood into the stock.

Put the bones, heads and tails into a large stock pot and add the cold water (see Note). Cover the pot and bring the water to a boil over high heat. Skim off any foam or fat that rises to the surface.

Add the remaining ingredients and bring to a boil. Lower the heat and simmer the stock for 30 minutes.

Strain the stock through a fine mesh strainer. Discard the bones, etc. and let cool. Store in small containers in the refrigerator or freezer.

NOTE: Shrimp shells can also be added to the stock for extra flavor.

PASTE E SALSE

Pasta and Pasta Sauces

Every summer Ciro hired a group of teenagers, including his four children and the children of friends, to do the prep work in his kitchen. Stephen Kinzer started out in the kitchen and then moved on to cashier. Years later, Stephen became campaign manager for Governor Dukakis of Massachusetts, and introduced the Governor and his wife to the restaurant. The Dukakis's have since become friends of Ciro and Patti and whenever the Governor is on the Cape, he has dinner at the restaurant. Stephen Kinzer has gone on to become the Latin American correspondent for The New York Times.

Things were still in their infancy when I made my first visit to Ciro & Sal's. The place had only been open for a month, but I was just two weeks old myself and didn't mind the chaos.

As a street urchin, I spent my mornings selling shells on Commercial Street and diving for coins that tourists tossed from MacMillan Wharf. Early each afternoon, I would slip into the kitchen at Ciro's— the restaurant was not yet open—and nonchalantly slice myself a thick hunk of Italian bread. I would present it to the man himself, who ceremoniously dunked it in his giant, simmering pot of tomato sauce and returned it to me. No urchin ever ate better.

Some evenings, long after I should have been in bed, my mother took me to Ciro's after closing time. Sitting on padded kegs and listening to the proprietors and their iconoclastic coterie discuss life and art while Italian arias played in the background, I learned great lessons early.

Many people you've heard of find their way to Ciro's, but I only heard the kitchen hush once. That was the night a waiter brought in an order for our best steak. "Make it a good one," he said. "It's for John Wayne."

In the ensuing years, I have shared Ciro's magic with appreciative guests throughout the hemisphere. A Sandinista *comandante* is the latest to ask for the sauce recipe.

—STEPHEN KINZER

◆————————◆

*T*hrice-elected selectman of Provincetown Monroe Moore and his wife Mary have two daughters who were born while the Moores lived in the "Alley." The Moores regularly ate at the restaurant and joked with waiter Al DiLauro, calling him Al Burro. Their daughters thought that Ciro was very kind to name a spaghetti after one of his employees. Years later, when they were in their teens, the girls discovered that Al's name was actually DiLauro. It was their greatest disillusionment since Santa Claus.

◆————————◆

SPAGHETTI AL BURRO E FORMAGGIO
Spaghetti with Butter and Cheese

SERVES 4 TO 6

1	pound spaghetti
12	tablespoons sweet butter
1	teaspoon pressed garlic
2	tablespoons finely chopped fresh basil leaves
4	tablespoons finely chopped fresh parsley leaves
3	tablespoons freshly grated Pecorino romano
	Freshly ground black pepper

Cook the spaghetti in salted boiling water until it is *al dente*.

While the spaghetti is cooking, melt the butter in a skillet. Add the garlic and lower the heat.

Drain the spaghetti and add it to the butter and garlic in the skillet. Toss quickly. Add the remaining ingredients and toss again. Serve at once.

SPAGHETTI CON AGLIO, OLIO E LIMONE
Spaghetti with Garlic, Oil and Lemon

SERVES 4 TO 6

1	pound spaghetti
⅔	cup extra virgin olive oil
6	garlic cloves, finely chopped
	Salt and freshly ground black pepper
1	lemon, quartered

Cook the spaghetti in salted boiling water until it is *al dente*.

While the spaghetti is cooking, heat the oil in a skillet and sauté the garlic over very low heat until it becomes a rich golden brown.

Drain the spaghetti and add it to the oil and garlic in the skillet. Add the salt and pepper and toss again. Serve immediately garnished with the lemon wedges.

SPAGHETTI CON FUNGHI
Spaghetti with Mushrooms

SERVES 4 TO 6

4 tablespoons butter
1½ cups thinly sliced mushrooms
2 teaspoons pressed garlic
4 tablespoons dry white wine
1½ cups Ragù (page 88)
1 pound spaghetti or linguine
Freshly grated Parmigiano

Melt the butter in a skillet. Add the mushrooms, and sauté them for 1 minute. Add the garlic and wine and continue to cook until the mushrooms are tender. Add the Ragù to the pan and heat slowly.

Cook the spaghetti in salted boiling water until it is *al dente*. Drain the spaghetti and transfer it to a warm serving bowl. Pour the sauce over the spaghetti and toss rapidly. Serve immediately with the grated Parmigiano.

SPAGHETTI CON PEPERONI

Spaghetti with Peppers

SERVES 4 TO 6

1	*pound spaghetti*
4	*sweet green peppers*
3	*tablespoons olive oil*
2	*teaspoons pressed garlic*
1½	*cups Ragù (page 88)*
	Freshly grated Parmigiano

Preheat oven to 400 degrees.

Wash and dry the peppers. Put the oil and garlic in a baking pan and roll the peppers in the oil, being sure to coat the peppers completely. Bake, uncovered, until the skins blister, turning them occasionally. Remove the peppers from the oven and put them in a paper bag; close the bag tightly. Let the peppers steam for 5 minutes; then peel, core and seed them under cold running water. Slice the peppers into ½-inch-wide strips.

Heat the Ragù slowly. Add the peppers to the sauce and continue heating for 10 minutes.

While the sauce is cooking, cook the spaghetti in salted boiling water until it is *al dente*.

Drain the spaghetti and transfer it to a warm serving bowl. Pour the sauce over the pasta, toss quickly and serve immediately with grated Parmigiano.

S*al and Josephine spent their honeymoon at his parents' birthplace, an island off the coast of Naples. It was in Foria, Ischia, that they tasted an unusual spaghetti served during Lent. Back in Provincetown, he and Ciro tried to re-create the spaghetti with a sauce made of anchovies. They continued to experiment, adding new ingredients until they finally created what is now known as* Spaghetti alla Foriana, *a house favorite to this day.*

I write during Lent, 1986. I am reminded of one of my favorite dishes anywhere, a traditional Italian Lenten dish called Spaghetti alla Foriana, *which I first encountered at* "Ciro and Sal's" *decades ago. I still order it there, decades later, along with whatever else pleases me. The restaurant's basic character is that of a civilized "bistro," the kind of restaurant that most artists love. . . .*

Apart from his lovable restaurant, Ciro Cozzi deserves the gratitude of the art community in Provincetown for his continual generosity, good will and empathy toward the arts which has manifested itself over many years in scores of ways, large and small. What a marvelous friend and neighbor!

—ROBERT MOTHERWELL

SPAGHETTI ALLA FORIANA

Spaghetti with Nuts, Raisins and Anchovies

SERVES 4 TO 6

1   *pound spaghetti*
¾   *cup extra virgin olive oil*
4   *garlic cloves, finely chopped*
12   *anchovy fillets, rinsed and dried*
½   *cup walnuts, broken into quarters*
¼   *cup pine nuts, lightly toasted*
½   *cup dark raisins*
1   *teaspoon dried oregano*
        Pinch of hot red pepper flakes
        Pinch of freshly ground black pepper
4   *tablespoons finely chopped fresh parsley leaves*

Cook the spaghetti in salted boiling water until it is *al dente*.

While the spaghetti is cooking, heat the oil in a deep skillet. Add the garlic and 9 of the anchovy fillets and sauté over low heat until the garlic is golden and the anchovies have dissolved (mash them with a fork). Add the walnuts, pine nuts, raisins, oregano, and black and red pepper and simmer for 4 minutes.

Drain the spaghetti and add it to the anchovy mixture in the pan. Add 3 tablespoons of the parsley and toss quickly.

Transfer the pasta to a warm serving bowl and garnish with the remaining anchovy fillets and parsley.

SPAGHETTI ALLA CARBONARA

Spaghetti with Pancetta, Eggs and Cream

SERVES 4 TO 6

½   pound pancetta, diced
3   large eggs, beaten
½   cup heavy cream
2   tablespoons freshly grated Parmigiano
1   teaspoon finely chopped fresh parsley leaves
    Freshly ground black pepper
1   pound spaghetti

Fry the pancetta in a large skillet until it is slightly crispy but not tough. Drain the fat from the pan.

Beat together the eggs, milk, cheese, parsley and black pepper.

Cook the spaghetti in salted boiling water until it is *al dente*. Drain the spaghetti and add it to the pancetta in the pan. Add the egg mixture. Cook briefly over very low heat, tossing to coat all the spaghetti with the egg. Do not overcook; the sauce should remain creamy.

Serve immediately with extra grated Parmigiano.

◆————————◆

F*or many years when prostitution was legal in Italy (it was outlawed in 1958), the busy Neapolitan prostitutes made Spaghetti alla Puttanesca. Some say this was because the sauce could be prepared quickly; others say it was because the strong aroma lured potential customers. I think both could be right.*

◆————————◆

SPAGHETTI ALLA PUTTANESCA
Spaghetti of the Whores

SERVES 4 TO 6

1	pound spaghetti
¼	cup olive oil
3	garlic cloves, finely chopped
1	1 pound, 12 ounce can plum tomatoes, drained, seeded and coarsely chopped
1	tablespoon capers, rinsed and drained
15	pitted black olives, thinly sliced
2	ounces anchovy fillets, rinsed, drained and chopped (about 16 fillets)
½ to 1	dried chili pepper, finely chopped
1	teaspoon dried basil
1	teaspoon dried oregano
2	tablespoons finely chopped fresh parsley leaves

Heat the oil in a large saucepan. Add the garlic and sauté until it is golden. Do not burn.

Add all the remaining ingredients except the parsley, and cook slowly for 15 minutes.

While the sauce is simmering, cook the spaghetti in salted boiling water until it is *al dente*.

Drain the spaghetti and transfer it to a warm serving bowl. Pour the sauce over the spaghetti and toss quickly. Sprinkle with the chopped parsley. Serve immediately.

NOTE: This spaghetti is wonderful with calamari (squid). Clean one dozen squid and slice them into thin rings. Use the tentacles also but keep them whole. Add the squid to the sauce and cook until tender (about 15 minutes). Pour over the cooked spaghetti and toss quickly.

SPAGHETTI CON SALSICCIA

Spaghetti with Sausages

SERVES 4 TO 6

6 to 8 *Italian sweet sausages*
½   *cup water*
1½   *cups Ragù (page 88)*
1   *pound spaghetti*
       Freshly grated Parmigiano

Preheat the oven to 400 degrees.

Put the sausages in a baking pan just large enough to hold them in one layer. Add the water, cover with aluminum foil and bake until cooked, 20 to 30 minutes.

Remove the sausages from the pan and add them to a saucepan with the Ragù. Heat slowly.

Cook the spaghetti in salted boiling water until it is *al dente.* Drain the spaghetti and transfer it to a warm serving bowl. Pour most of the Ragù over the spaghetti and toss quickly. Serve the sausages in the remaining sauce on a separate dish. Serve immediately with the grated Parmigiano.

SPAGHETTI CON VONGOLE IN BIANCO
Spaghetti with Clams

SERVES 4 TO 6

32	cherrystone clams (about 8 pounds total weight)
1	pound spaghetti or linguine
⅔	cup olive oil
5	garlic cloves, finely chopped
1	tablespoon chopped fresh basil leaves
½	teaspoon dried oregano
½	teaspoon hot red pepper flakes
2	tablespoons finely chopped fresh parsley leaves

To facilitate opening the clams, place them on a tray and put them into a very hot oven for 2 minutes. Open the clams, remove the meat and reserve the juice. Cut each clam into two or three pieces.

Cook the spaghetti in salted boiling water until it is *al dente*.

While the spaghetti is cooking, heat the oil in a skillet. Add the garlic and sauté until it is golden. Add the reserved clam juice, basil, oregano and pepper flakes and bring to a boil. Add the clams and 1½ tablespoons of the parsley. Cook over moderate heat just until the clams are hot.

Drain the spaghetti and transfer it to a warm serving bowl. Pour the clam sauce over the spaghetti and toss quickly. Sprinkle with the remaining parsley and serve immediately.

PASTA ALL 'ABRUZZESE
Pasta with Seafood, Tomatoes and Herbs

SERVES 4

¼ cup olive oil
3 garlic cloves, finely chopped
1 onion, finely chopped
3 cups imported Italian plum tomatoes, peeled, seeded and chopped
½ cup fish stock (page 52)
2 tablespoons dry white wine
1 tablespoon chopped fresh basil leaves
¼ teaspoon hot red pepper flakes
½ pound boneless and skinless haddock or cod
4 mussels, scrubbed and debearded
8 shrimp, peeled and deveined
4 littleneck clams, washed
2 squid, cleaned and cut into rings
3 tablespoons finely chopped fresh parsley leaves
1 pound spaghetti or linguine

Heat the oil in a large saucepan. Add the garlic and onions and sauté until the onion is translucent.

Add the tomatoes, stock, wine, basil and hot pepper flakes to the pan. Simmer for 20 minutes.

Transfer 1 cup of this sauce to another saucepan and poach the haddock in it. Do not overcook the fish.

At the same time, add the remaining seafood and 2 tablespoons of the parsley to the sauce. Cover and cook for 10 minutes, or until all the seafood is cooked. Leave the clams and mussels in their shells.

While the seafood is cooking, cook the spaghetti in salted boiling water until it is *al dente*. Drain the spaghetti and transfer it to a warm serving bowl.

Place the haddock in the center of the spaghetti and surround it with the other seafood. Pour the sauce over the spaghetti and sprinkle with the remaining parsley.

PASTA CON SALSA DI NOCI
Pasta with Walnut Sauce

SERVES 4 TO 6

1	pound linguine or fettuccine
1	cup walnuts, chopped
⅓	cup blanched almonds, toasted and chopped
2	garlic cloves, chopped
2	tablespoons fresh marjoram, chopped
¼	cup fresh parsley, chopped
¼	cup fresh basil leaves, chopped
6	tablespoons whole milk ricotta
2	tablespoons freshly grated Pecorino romano
½	cup extra virgin olive oil
	Salt and freshly ground black pepper
12 to 18	whole walnut halves, toasted
	Freshly grated Pecorino romano

Cook the pasta in salted boiling water until it is *al dente*.

While the pasta is cooking, combine the remaining ingredients in a food processor or blender and blend until smooth. Heat the sauce over very low heat.

Drain the pasta, leaving it slightly wet, and transfer it to a warm serving bowl. Add the walnut sauce and toss well. Do not add all of the sauce if there is too much; this should not be a heavy dish.

Serve immediately with additional freshly grated Pecorino romano and toasted whole walnuts—3 per serving.

This sauce is also excellent with tortellini.

*If a slightly thinner or creamier sauce is desired, add a little heavy cream to the sauce as you heat it.

LINGUINE ALLA FIGLIA

Linguine with Piquant Tomato Sauce and Goat Cheese

SERVES 4 TO 6

3	tablespoons olive oil
3	garlic cloves, finely chopped
½	carrot, finely chopped
1	celery stalk, finely chopped
1	small onion, finely chopped
2	anchovy fillets, rinsed, dried and chopped
8	sun-dried tomatoes, soaked for 30 minutes in tepid water, and then drained and rinsed
¼	cup dry red wine
1	1-pound can imported Italian plum tomatoes
1	bay leaf
1	teaspoon chopped fresh basil leaves
1	teaspoon chopped fresh rosemary leaves
2	teaspoons chopped fresh parsley leaves
	Salt and freshly ground black pepper
	Dash of red wine vinegar
	Pinch of hot red pepper flakes
1	pound linguine
4	tablespoons butter, cut into small pieces and at room temperature (optional)
4	ounces mild goat cheese, broken up (optional)
	Freshly grated Parmigiano

Heat the oil in a heavy saucepan. Add the garlic, carrot, celery and onion and sauté until the vegetables are tender. Add the anchovies and sun-dried tomatoes. Mash them with a fork until they dissolve.

Pass the contents of the pan through a large mesh sieve (to remove the tomato skins). Return the purée to the pan and add the wine. Let the wine reduce to about 3 tablespoons.

Pass the tomatoes through a sieve to remove the seeds. Add the tomatoes, bay leaf, basil, rosemary and parsley to the pan. Simmer over very low heat for 2 hours. Add the vinegar and hot pepper flakes. Season with salt and pepper.

Cook the linguine in boiling salted water until it is *al dente*. Drain and transfer it to a warm serving bowl. If desired, add the butter and toss quickly to melt. Add the goat cheese and toss, then pour the sauce over the pasta (reserve ¼ cup) and toss again. Pour the remaining sauce on top.

Serve immediately with freshly grated Parmigiano.

LINGUINE ESTIVE

Summertime Linguine

SERVES 4 TO 6

1	*pound linguine*
¾	*cup extra virgin olive oil*
4	*garlic cloves, sliced*
4	*large ripe tomatoes, cut into ¼-inch wedges*
10	*fresh basil leaves, stems removed*
	Salt and freshly ground black pepper
1	*pound fresh mozzarella, cut into small cubes and at room temperature*

Cook the linguine in boiling salted water until it is *al dente*.

Heat the oil in a heavy skillet. Add the garlic and sauté until it is golden brown. Remove the garlic and discard. Lower the heat and add the tomatoes, basil, salt and pepper. Cook for 1 minute.

Drain the linguine and transfer it to a warm serving bowl. Pour the sauce over the linguine and toss quickly but well. Add the mozzarella and toss again. Serve immediately.

LINGUINE CON PESTO
Linguine with Basil and Garlic
SERVES 4 TO 6

1   *pound linguine*
1   *recipe for Pesto (page 89), at room temperature*
     Freshly grated Parmigiano
     Toasted pine nuts

Cook the linguine in salted boiling water until it is *al dente*. Drain the pasta leaving it slightly wet. Transfer it to a saucepan and add the Pesto. Toss quickly over very low heat, then transfer the linguine to a warm serving bowl and sprinkle it with the grated Parmigiano and pine nuts.

NOTE: An alternate method is to heat the Pesto slightly first. Drain the cooked linguine and transfer it to a warm serving bowl. Add the Pesto to the linguine and toss rapidly to distribute the Pesto evenly over the linguine. Sprinkle with the Parmigiano and toasted pine nuts. Serve immediately.

FETTUCCINE ALL' ANDREA
Fettuccine with Zucchini and Mushrooms in Cream Sauce
SERVES 4 TO 6

1   *pound fettuccine*
6   *tablespoons butter*
1½   *cups thinly sliced mushrooms*
2   *small zucchini, cut into ⅛-inch julienne (may use food processor)*
1   *large carrot, peeled and cut to match the zucchini*
1½   *cups heavy cream*
     Salt and freshly ground black pepper
½   *cup freshly grated Parmigiano*

Melt 3 tablespoons of the butter in a skillet. Add the mushrooms, carrots and zucchini and cook until tender.

Cook the fettuccine in salted boiling water until it is *al dente*.

In a large skillet, heat the cream over low heat. Add the butter, vegetables, salt and pepper. Heat slowly.

Drain the pasta and add it to the cream mixture in the pan. Add the Parmigiano and toss quickly to coat the pasta.

Serve immediately with additional Parmigiano and black pepper.

FETTUCCINE CON PESTO E PANNA

Fettuccine with Pesto and Cream

SERVES 4 TO 6

1	*pound fettuccine*
1	*recipe for Pesto (page 89)*
1½	*cups heavy cream*
	Salt and freshly ground black pepper
	Freshly grated Parmigiano
	Toasted pine nuts

Cook the fettuccine in salted boiling water until it is *al dente*. While the fettuccine is cooking, prepare the sauce. Heat the Pesto in a large skillet and add the cream, salt and pepper (see Note). Whisk over high heat until smooth and creamy.

Drain the fettuccine and transfer it to a warm serving bowl. Pour the sauce over the fettuccine and toss well. Sprinkle with the Parmigiano and pine nuts and serve immediately.

NOTE: Freshly grated nutmeg may also be added to the sauce.

FETTUCCINE ALLA ROMANA

Fettuccine with Cream and Parmigiano

SERVES 4 TO 6

1	*pound fettuccine*
1½	*cups heavy cream*
16	*tablespoons sweet butter*
	Scant pinch of freshly grated nutmeg
	Salt and freshly ground black pepper
⅔	*cup freshly grated Parmigiano*

Cook the fettuccine in salted boiling water until it is *al dente*.

While the fettuccine is cooking, heat the cream, butter, nutmeg, salt and pepper over very low heat. Whisk constantly for 1 minute.

Drain the noodles and add them to the sauce in the pan. Sprinkle with the Parmigiano and toss quickly to coat all the noodles.

Serve immediately with additional grated Parmigiano and black pepper.

FETTUCCINE CON GORGONZOLA
Fettuccine with Gorgonzola

SERVES 4 TO 6

1   pound fettuccine
½   cup clarified butter (page 223)
4   garlic cloves, finely chopped
¼   cup dry white wine
½   cup chicken stock (page 51)
1   cup chopped, peeled and seeded tomatoes
8   fresh basil leaves, stems removed
4   ounces Gorgonzola (the soft variety) broken into small pieces
1   cup light cream
2   ounces freshly grated Parmigiano
    Salt and freshly ground black pepper
¼   cup pine nuts, toasted

Cook the fettuccine in boiling salted water until it is *al dente*.

While it is cooking, prepare the sauce. Heat the butter in a very large skillet. Add the garlic and sauté for 30 seconds. Raise the heat, add the white wine and let it reduce to about 3 tablespoons. Add the stock and let reduce for 1 to 2 minutes. Add the tomatoes, basil and gorgonzola. Lower the heat and stir rapidly to melt the cheese. Add the cream, salt and pepper. Raise the heat and let the sauce reduce for 1 minute more. Lower the heat.

Drain the fettuccine and add it to the sauce in the pan. Toss well to coat all the noodles with the sauce, then remove from the heat. Add half of the grated cheese and all but 2 tablespoons of the pine nuts and toss again.

Serve immediately with the extra grated Parmigiano and pine nuts sprinkled on top.

NOTE: For a different but equally delicious dish, omit the tomatoes and basil.

FETTUCCINE CON FORMAGGIO E PROSCIUTTO

Fettuccine with Cheese and Prosciutto

SERVES 4 TO 6

1   *pound fettuccine*
¼   *cup clarified butter (page 223)*
2   *garlic cloves, finely chopped*
¼   *cup dry white wine*
½   *cup chicken stock (page 51)*
2   *ounces fontina, grated*
2   *ounces ricotta*
1   *cup light cream*
6   *slices prosciutto, trimmed of fat, cut into ¼-inch pieces*
     Salt and freshly ground black pepper
2   *ounces freshly grated Parmigiano*

Cook the fettuccine in boiling salted water until it is *al dente*.

While the fettuccine is cooking, prepare the sauce. Heat the butter in a large skillet. Add the garlic and sauté for 30 seconds (do not burn it). Raise the heat and add the wine. Let the wine reduce to about 3 tablespoons. Add the stock and let it reduce again for 1 to 2 minutes. Lower the heat, add the cheeses and stir until they are melted. Add the cream, prosciutto, salt and pepper. Let reduce for 1 minute. Lower the heat.

Drain the fettuccine and add it to the sauce in the pan. Toss well to coat all the noodles. Sprinkle with the grated Parmigiano and toss again. Serve immediately.

FETTUCCINE CON SALMONE E TARTUFI
Fettuccine with Salmon and Truffles

SERVES 4

1	cup fish stock (page 52)
1	cup shrimp shells, if available
1	pound fettuccine
2	tablespoons brandy
2	bay leaves
1	cup heavy cream
1	tablespoon white or black truffles, thinly sliced or shaved
8	fresh basil leaves, stems removed
½	pound smoked salmon, cut into thin strips
1	large egg yolk
	Salt and freshly ground white pepper

Combine the stock and shrimp shells in a saucepan and bring to a boil. Lower the heat and simmer for 15 minutes. Strain out the shells and return the stock to the pan.

Cook the fettuccine in boiling salted water until it is *al dente*.

While the fettuccine is cooking, finish the sauce. Add the brandy, bay leaves, truffles (reserve a couple for garnish) and cream to the stock. Let the sauce reduce for 2 minutes. Add 12 strips of the salmon and 6 of the basil leaves. Then whisk in the egg yolk and season with salt and pepper.

Drain the fettuccine and transfer it to a warm serving bowl. Pour the sauce over the fettuccine and toss well. Garnish with the extra salmon, basil and truffles. Serve immediately.

PENNE ALL' ARRABBIATA
Angry Penne
SERVES 4 TO 6

4 to 6 *tablespoons olive oil*
2   *garlic cloves, finely chopped or pressed*
2   *ounces pancetta*
1½   *cups Italian plum tomatoes, passed through a sieve*
2   *parsley sprigs*
       Pinch of hot red pepper flakes or a small piece of dried red pepper
       Salt
1   *pound penne*
2   *ounces Pecorino, grated*
       Freshly grated Parmigiano

Heat the oil in a nonstick saucepan. Add the garlic and sauté over low heat for 1 minute. Raise the heat slightly, add the pancetta and brown on both sides. Add the tomatoes, parsley, hot pepper flakes and salt. Cover and cook over moderate heat for 20 minutes. Discard the meat and parsley.

In the meantime, cook the penne in salted boiling water until it is *al dente.*

Drain the penne and add it to the sauce in the pan. Add the grated Pecorino and cook for 2 minutes over high heat, tossing the penne to coat it with the sauce. Serve immediately with the grated Parmigiano.

TORTELLINI CON PANNA

Tortellini with Cream

SERVES 4

60   *tortellini*
4   *tablespoons butter*
2   *tablespoons brandy*
1½ *cups heavy cream*
½   *teaspoon freshly grated nutmeg*
2   *large egg yolks*
6   *tablespoons freshly grated Parmigiano*
    Salt and freshly ground white pepper

Cook the tortellini in salted boiling water (see Glossary for cooking times).

While the tortellini is cooking, prepare the sauce. Melt the butter in a heavy skillet. Raise the heat, add the brandy and let it burn off. Add the cream and nutmeg and reduce for 1 minute.

Drain the tortellini and transfer it to a warm serving bowl.

Whisk the egg yolks and 4 tablespoons of the grated Parmigiano into the sauce. Season with salt and pepper. Pour the sauce over the tortellini, sprinkle with the remaining Parmigiano and serve immediately.

LASAGNE AL FORNO

Lasagne with Ragù and Cheese

SERVES 6

1	tablespoon olive oil
	Salt
13	strips curly edged lasagne noodles
4	cups Ragù (page 88)
1	pound ground beef, sautéed or made into marble-size meatballs. (Use the polpette recipe, page 154, but omit the raisins.)
¾	pound Italian sweet sausages, cooked and thinly sliced
1 to 1½	pounds whole milk ricotta, drained of excess liquid
½	pound whole milk mozzarella, finely chopped
5	tablespoons freshly grated Parmigiano
4	hard-boiled large eggs, chopped
1	cup Balsamella (page 192)
	Freshly ground black pepper

Bring a large pot of water to a boil. Add the oil and a generous amount of salt to the water. Cook the lasagne until they are *al dente*. Drain and cool in cold water, then pat them dry with paper towels. Lay the noodles in a single layer on a cloth towel, but do not overlap them.

Preheat the oven to 375 degrees.

Cover the bottom of a 9- by 13- by 2-inch baking pan with a thin layer of the Ragù. Lay 5 strips of noodles along the width of the pan. Spread half of all the remaining ingredients in layers over the noodles. Pour a generous amount of the Ragù and ½ cup of the Balsamella over the ingredients (do not flood with sauce).

Lay 3 strips of noodles lengthwise over the first layer. Spread the remaining half of the ingredients in layers over the noodles. Reserve some Parmigiano. Cover with some of the Ragù and the remaining Balsamella.

Layer the remaining noodles along the width of the pan. Pour the remaining Ragù over the noodles and sprinkle with the Parmigiano.

Cover the pan with aluminum foil and bake for 25 minutes. Remove the foil and bake for 10 minutes more. Let stand for 5 minutes before serving.

LASAGNE VERDI

Spinach Lasagne with Four Cheeses

SERVES 6

1	tablespoon olive oil
	Salt
13	strips curly edged spinach lasagne
3	tablespoons butter, melted
2½	pounds whole milk ricotta, drained of excess liquid
½	pound whole milk mozzarella, finely chopped
6	hard-boiled large eggs, chopped
¾	cup fresh grated Parmigiano
¾	cup fresh grated Pecorino romano
1½	cups Balsamella (page 192)
4	large eggs, beaten
	Freshly ground black pepper

Bring a large pot of water to a boil. Add the oil and a generous amount of salt. Cook the lasagne until they are *al dente*. Drain and cool in cold water, then pat them dry with paper towels. Lay the noodles in a single layer on a cloth towel, but do not overlap them.

Preheat the oven to 375 degrees.

Brush the bottom of a 9- by 13- by 2-inch baking pan with 1½ tablespoons of the butter. Arrange the layers of noodles as in the recipe for Lasagne al Forno. Spread half of the remaining ingredients on the 2 layers. (Reserve some Parmigiano.) Brush the final layer with the remaining butter and sprinkle with the grated Parmigiano.

Cover the pan with aluminum foil and bake for 25 minutes. Remove the foil and continue baking for 5 minutes. Let stand for 5 minutes before serving. If desired, spread with extra Balsamella before serving.

LASAGNE ALLA VENEZIANA

Spinach Lasagne Layered with Broccoli, Zucchini, Veal and Chicken

SERVES 6

1   tablespoon olive oil
     Salt
13   strips curly edged spinach lasagne
1½   tablespoons melted butter
1½   pounds whole milk ricotta, drained of excess liquid
2   cups chopped broccoli flowerets
1½   cups chopped zucchini
1   cup thinly sliced fresh mushrooms
1   cup freshly grated Pecorino romano
½   pound cooked chicken, chopped
½   pound ground veal, sautéed
½   cup Balsamella (page 192)
1½   cups Espagnole Sauce (page 195)
     Freshly ground black pepper

Bring a large pot of water to a boil. Add the olive oil and a generous amount of salt. Cook the lasagne until they are *al dente*. Drain and cool in cold water, then pat them dry with paper towels. Lay the noodles in a single layer on a cloth towel, but do not overlap them.

Preheat the oven to 375 degrees.

Brush the bottom of a 9- by 13- by 2-inch baking pan with the melted butter. Arrange the noodles as in the recipe for Lasagne al Forno. Spread half of all the ingredients on the 2 layers. Reserve ½ cup of the Espagnole Sauce.

Pour the remaining Espagnole Sauce over the top of the lasagne. Cover with aluminum foil and bake for 25 minutes. Remove the foil and bake 5 minutes more. Let stand for 5 minutes before serving.

Serve with additional Balsamella and Espagnole sauces if desired.

CRESPELLE

Crêpes

MAKES 18 CRESPELLE

5   large eggs
1½   cups milk
1   cup water
2   cups all-purpose flour
½   teaspoon salt
½   cup vegetable oil

In a mixing bowl, beat together the eggs, milk, water and salt with a wire whisk. Add the flour a little at a time, beating until thoroughly blended. Cover the batter and refrigerate for 2 hours.

Heat an 8-inch crêpe pan. Rub the bottom of the pan with a paper towel dipped in vegetable oil.

Pour about ¼ cup of the batter into the pan. Tilt the pan immediately so that the batter spreads over the entire bottom of the pan. Cook the crespelle quickly on one side only. Remove the crespelle from the pan by turning the pan over onto a plate. Stack the crespelle and keep covered until ready to use.

CRESPELLE VERDI

Spinach Crêpes

MAKES 18 CRESPELLE

2   cups fresh spinach, leaves only
    Pinch salt
1   recipe for crespelle batter

Carefully wash the spinach and leave it wet. Lightly steam the spinach in its own water, adding a pinch of salt.

When the spinach has wilted, drain it and squeeze out all the excess liquid, then chop it finely.

Mix the spinach together with 1 cup of the batter. Then mix this into the remaining batter.

Cook as for regular crespelle.

◆————————◆

O*ne day in the late fifties saladman Dan Bernstein's mother came to the restaurant and made blintzes for the help. After watching her make the crêpes, Ciro and Sal got the idea to use these same crêpes instead of pasta to make manicotti. They worked wonderfully and are now used in several dishes.*

◆————————◆

MANICOTTI

Stuffed Crêpes with Black Olives and Prosciutto

SERVES 6

2	pounds whole milk ricotta
1	large egg
1	cup freshly grated Parmigiano
¼	cup finely chopped walnuts
¼	cup blanched slivered almonds
½	cup finely chopped black olives
½	cup finely chopped fresh parsley leaves
1	tablespoon dried basil or finely chopped fresh basil leaves
	Salt and freshly ground black pepper
12	thin slices prosciutto, trimmed of excess fat
12	crespelle (page 79)
12	thin slices whole milk mozzarella
2	cups Ragú (page 88)

Preheat the oven to 450 degrees.

In a large mixing bowl combine the ricotta, eggs, ½ cup of the Parmigiano, walnuts, almonds, olives, parsley, basil, salt and pepper. Mix well.

Lay the crespelle, browned side up, on work surface.

Place 1 slice of prosciutto on each crespelle. Top with a large scoop of the ricotta mixture (about ¼ cup). Fold half of the crespella over the cheese, fold in the sides and then fold over the other half. The manicotti will be tubular shaped.

Spread half of the sauce over the bottom of a large baking pan. Arrange the manicotti, seam side up, in the pan. Cover with the remaining sauce. Be careful not to drown the manicotti in sauce.

Cover the pan with aluminum foil and bake for 15 minutes. Remove the foil, cover each roll with a slice of mozzarella and sprinkle all with the remaining Parmigiano. Return to the oven, uncovered, for 5 minutes, or until the cheese has melted. Serve immediately.

MANICOTTI VERDI

Stuffed Spinach Crêpes with Chicken and Herbs

SERVES 6

2	pounds whole milk ricotta
1	pound fresh spinach
1	cup freshly grated Parmigiano
1	cup finely chopped fresh parsley leaves
1	large egg
2	cups cooked chicken, coarsely chopped (about 1 whole breast)
1	tablespoon chopped fresh basil leaves or dried basil
½	teaspoon dried marjoram
	Salt and freshly ground black pepper
12	crespelle verdi (page 80)
⅔	cup butter, melted
12	thin slices whole milk mozzarella

Preheat the oven to 450 degrees.

Using a double thickness of cheesecloth, squeeze any excess liquid from the ricotta.

Clean the spinach and leave it wet. Steam the spinach lightly in its own water with a little salt. Drain, squeeze out the excess water and chop the spinach finely.

In a large mixing bowl, combine the ricotta, ½ cup of the Parmigiano, spinach, parsley, egg, chicken, basil, marjoram, salt and pepper. Mix well.

Lay the crespelle, browned side up, on the work surface.

Place a large scoop of the ricotta mixture (about ¼ cup) onto each crespella. Fold half of the crespella over the cheese, fold in the sides and then fold over the other half.

Brush a large baking pan with melted butter. Arrange the manicotti seam side up in the pan and brush with melted butter.

Cover with aluminum foil and bake for 20 minutes. Remove the foil and top each roll with a slice of mozzarella and a sprinkle of grated Parmigiano. Return to the oven, uncovered, and bake for 5 minutes more, or until the cheese has melted. Serve immediately.

CANNELLONI ALLA GENOVESE
Seafood Cannelloni

SERVES 6

12	crespelle (page 79)
2	pounds shrimp, shelled (Reserve the shells.)
1	pound haddock or flounder
1	cup steamed mussels, shelled
1	cup bay scallops
¼	cup white wine
½	fresh lemon
6	large egg yolks
2	cups ricotta
1	cup finely chopped mozzarella
½	cup dry sherry
⅛	teaspoon cayenne pepper
½	teaspoon freshly grated nutmeg
½	cup finely chopped fresh parsley leaves
	Salt and freshly ground black pepper
3	cups fish stock (page 52)
3	bay leaves
½	cup dry white wine
1	cup heavy cream
1	teaspoon tomato paste
¼	teaspoon freshly grated nutmeg
	Salt and freshly ground white pepper

Preheat the oven to 450 degrees.

Poach the shrimp, scallops and haddock in water with the white wine and lemon. Drain and shock in ice water. Drain again. Chop the shrimp, fish and mussels. Combine all the seafood in a large bowl.

Add the egg yolks, ricotta, mozzarella, sherry, cayenne, nutmeg, parsley, salt and black pepper. Mix well.

Lay the crespelle, brown side up, on a work surface. Place a large scoop of the seafood mixture on each. Roll one end first, then the sides up over the filling. Fold over the remaining half. The cannelloni will be tubular shaped. Place them in a buttered baking pan. Cover with aluminum foil and bake for 15 to 20 minutes.

While the cannelloni is baking, prepare the sauce. Combine the stock, reserved shrimp shells, bay leaves and wine in a saucepan. Bring to a boil and simmer for 20 minutes. Strain the shells and bay leaves from the stock, and return it to the pan. Add the cream and reduce by ½. Dissolve the tomato paste in ½ cup of the sauce and add this to the pan. Season with nutmeg, salt and white pepper.

Cover the bottom of the serving plate with a little sauce. Arrange the cannelloni on top and pour a little more of the sauce over the cannelloni. Serve immediately.

CANNELLONI VERDI

Stuffed Spinach Crêpes with Veal, Pork and Chicken

SERVES 6

½   cup butter, melted
2   tablespoons dry sherry
1   pound ground veal
       Salt and freshly ground black pepper
½   pound ground pork
½   pound spinach
1   cup coarsely chopped cooked chicken (about ½ breast)
1   pound whole milk ricotta, drained of excess liquid
1   large egg
1½   tablespoons dried basil or chopped fresh basil leaves
1½   teaspoons pressed garlic
½   teaspoon dried thyme
½   cup freshly grated Parmigiano
½   cup finely chopped fresh parsley
12   crespelle verdi (see recipe)
1   cup Balsamella (page 192)
½   cup Espagnole Sauce (page 195)

Preheat the oven to 450 degrees.

Heat a little of the butter in a frying pan and sauté the veal with the sherry until it is just done. Season with salt and pepper. Remove the veal to a large mixing bowl.

In the same pan, heat more of the butter and sauté the pork until it is just done. Season with salt and pepper. Add the pork to the veal.

Clean the spinach and leave it wet. Steam it lightly with its own water and a little salt. Drain, squeeze out the excess water and chop the spinach finely. Add it to the cooked meats.

Add all the remaining ingredients, except the crespelle, Balsamella and Espagnole Sauce to the meat and spinach. Mix thoroughly. Season with salt and pepper.

Lay the crespelle, browned side up, on the work surface.

Place a large scoop of the mixture (about ¼ cup) on each crespella. Fold as for Cannelloni alla Genovese.

Brush a large baking pan with melted butter. Arrange the cannelloni, seam side up, in the pan. Pour the Balsamella over the cannelloni and pour the Espagnole sauce over the Balsamella.

Cover with aluminum foil and bake for 20 minutes. Serve immediately.

SALSA DI POMODORO SEMPLICE

Simple Tomato Sauce

MAKES ENOUGH FOR 1 POUND OF PASTA

This is a tomato sauce that is very easy to make.

2	tablespoons olive oil
1	ounce pancetta, cut into thin strips
2	garlic cloves, sliced thin
	A tiny piece of dried red pepper or a pinch of hot red pepper flakes
1	pound Italian plum tomatoes, peeled and seeded
6	fresh basil leaves, chopped
2	parsley sprigs, leaves only
	Salt

Heat the olive oil in a saucepan. Add the pancetta and garlic, lower the heat and lightly brown both. Remove them from the pan and discard. Add the remaining ingredients and simmer for 30 minutes to 1 hour. Mash the tomatoes with a fork as they cook.

NOTE: For a thicker sauce, add a teaspoon of tomato paste.

CANNELLONI

Stuffed Crêpes with Chicken Livers and Mushrooms

SERVES 6

¼   cup butter, melted
1   pound ground veal
½   teaspoon dried thyme
1   tablespoon dried basil
2   tablespoons dry white wine
     Salt and freshly ground black pepper
     Juice of ½ lemon
½   pound ground beef
1   pound chicken livers, finely chopped
½   cup coarsely chopped cooked chicken (about ¼ breast)
½   cup finely chopped fresh mushrooms
1   pound whole milk ricotta, drained of excess liquid
1   large egg
½   cup freshly grated Parmigiano
½   cup finely chopped fresh parsley leaves
12   crespelle (see recipe for regular crespelle)
3   cups Ragù (page 88)

Heat a little of the butter in a frying pan and sauté the veal with the thyme, basil and wine. Add the lemon juice to the veal once it is cooked. Season with salt and pepper. Remove the veal to a large mixing bowl.

Preheat the oven to 450 degrees.

In the same frying pan, heat a little more butter and sauté the beef until it is just done. Season with salt and pepper.

Add the beef and all the remaining ingredients, except the crespelle and Ragù, to the veal, and mix thoroughly. Season with salt and pepper.

Lay the crespella, browned side up, on the work surface.

Place a large scoop of the veal mixture (about ¼ cup) onto each crespella. Roll as for Cannelloni alla Genovese.

Spread half of the Ragù sauce over the bottom of a large baking pan. Arrange the cannelloni, seam side up, in the pan. Cover with the remaining sauce. Be careful not to drown the cannelloni in sauce. Cover with aluminum foil and bake for 25 minutes. Serve immediately with extra grated Parmigiano.

SALSA MARINARA

Tomato and Vegetable Sauce

MAKES 1 QUART

3 *tablespoons olive oil*
2 *garlic cloves, chopped finely*
1 *onion, chopped*
½ *celery stalk, sliced on an angle*
1 *2-pound, 3-ounce can imported Italian tomatoes, seeded and*
     coarsely chopped
½ *cup dry white wine*
1 *tablespoon red wine vinegar*
1 *bay leaf*
½ *teaspoon dried rosemary or chopped fresh rosemary leaves*
1 *teaspoon dried oregano*
1 *tablespoon dried basil, or fresh basil leaves*
½ *sweet green pepper, chopped*
10 *pitted black olives, chopped*
     Pinch of hot red pepper flakes
1 *teaspoon salt*
½ *teaspoon freshly ground black pepper*
2 *tablespoons finely chopped fresh parsley leaves*

Heat the oil in a saucepan. Add the garlic, onions and celery, and sauté until the onion and garlic are lightly browned.

Add all the other ingredients and bring to a boil. Lower the heat and simmer for 25 minutes.

Use immediately or cool completely and refrigerate.

RAGÙ

Meat Sauce

MAKES 3½ QUARTS

¼   cup olive oil
1½ pounds each veal and beef bones
½   pound salt pork
5   garlic cloves, finely chopped
2   carrots, finely chopped
4   onions, finely chopped
2   celery stalks, finely chopped
2   1-pound, 12-ounce cans Italian plum tomatoes, seeded and
      coarsely chopped
1   1-pound, 12-ounce can tomato purée
2   6-ounce cans tomato paste
1   cup dry red wine
1   cup water
2   tablespoons dried basil
2   bay leaves
½   teaspoon hot red pepper flakes
    Salt and freshly ground black pepper

Heat the oil in a large heavy saucepan. Add the bones and the salt pork and cook for 10 minutes, stirring occasionally. Remove bones and salt pork and discard.

Add the garlic to the pan and brown lightly, then add the onions, carrots and celery and sauté until the vegetables are tender.

Add all the remaining ingredients and bring to a boil. Lower the heat and simmer for 2 hours, stirring occasionally.

Refrigerate in airtight containers or freeze in small amounts.

RAGÙ II

Meat Sauce

MAKES ENOUGH FOR 1 POUND OF PASTA

¼   cup olive oil
10 ounces ground pork

3   ounces pancetta, ground
1   small onion, finely chopped
1   small carrot, peeled and finely chopped
1   celery stalk, finely chopped
1   garlic clove, finely chopped (optional)
1   cup meat broth (page 49)
1   heaping teaspoon tomato paste
     Salt and freshly ground black pepper

Heat the oil in a saucepan or large skillet. Add the ground pork, pancetta, onion, carrot, celery and garlic, and brown over high heat.

Add the broth and tomato paste and stir well over high heat. Season with salt and pepper, then cover the contents of the pan with cold water and bring to a boil. Lower the heat and simmer for 30 to 45 minutes.

NOTE: This sauce can be made extra special by adding a few shavings of fresh truffles and some grated Parmigiano just before serving.

PESTO

Basil and Garlic Sauce

MAKES ENOUGH FOR 1 POUND OF SPAGHETTI

2   cups fresh basil leaves without stems
¾   cup extra virgin olive oil
5   garlic cloves, peeled
2   tablespoons pine nuts (walnuts may be substituted)
⅔   cup freshly grated Parmigiano
     Salt and freshly ground black pepper

Combine all the ingredients in an electric blender or food processor. Blend on the highest speed until smooth.

If the Pesto is not to be used immediately, place it in a container and cover it with ½ inch of olive oil. Seal tightly. The Pesto may also be frozen in the same manner.

POLENTA E RISOTTI

Polenta and Rice

*G*andy Brody came into the restaurant one day and said, "I have a great proposition for you! I have to eat. You can feed me, and in exchange I will read stories to all the children that come in with their families to eat."

◆————————◆

POLENTA
Cornmeal

SERVES 4

6   cups veal, chicken or beef stock, (pages 50, 51, and 49) or
       water or milk
½   pound stone-ground yellow cornmeal
       Salt and freshly ground black pepper
2   tablespoons butter

Bring the stock to a boil in a heavy saucepan. The liquid you use will depend on which flavor you desire; it should complement the food it is to accompany.

Pour the cornmeal very slowly into the boiling liquid while stirring constantly with a wooden spoon. Lower the heat and cook the polenta for about 20 to 40 minutes, stirring constantly throughout the cooking period.

Season with salt and pepper, then stir in the butter.

90

Remove from the heat and transfer the polenta to a warm serving plate. Allow it to sit for 5 to 10 minutes. Slice or spoon it into portions and serve it with any very flavorful food. It will act as a perfect foil to strongly flavored dishes such as grilled or braised meats and fowl, squid with ink sauce, or grilled wild mushrooms (page 92).

Another option is to spread the polenta on a flat baking sheet. Allow the polenta to set until very firm. Slice it into rectangles and grill it. This, again, would be used as an accompaniment for strongly flavored or spicy foods.

If milk is used to make the polenta, it makes an excellent first course. It may be seasoned with fresh herbs and should be served with freshly grated Parmigiano.

POLENTA AI QUATTRO FORMAGGI
Polenta with Four Cheeses

SERVES 4

6   *cups chicken stock (page 51)*
½   *pound stone-ground yellow cornmeal*
1   *ounce fontina, cut into small cubes*
1   *ounce fresh mozzarella, cut into small cubes*
1   *ounce Gorgonzola (the soft variety)*
⅛   *cup freshly grated Parmigiano*
    Salt and freshly ground black pepper
2   *tablespoons butter, at room temperature*

Bring the chicken stock to a boil in a heavy saucepan. (If stock is not available, water may be substituted with excellent results.)

Pour the cornmeal very slowly into the boiling stock while stirring constantly with a wooden spoon. Lower the heat and cook the polenta for 30 minutes, stirring constantly throughout the cooking period.

Add the cheeses to the polenta and continue to stir. Cook the polenta until they have melted. Season with salt and pepper, then stir in the butter.

Remove from the heat and transfer the polenta to a warm serving plate. Serve immediately with extra grated Parmigiano. The polenta may be used as a first or main course.

POLENTA CON FUNGHI ALLA GRIGLIA
Polenta with Grilled Mushrooms

Prepare the polenta of your choice. Then clean any assortment of fresh, wild mushrooms. Coat them with a mixture of extra virgin olive oil, salt, freshly ground black pepper, chopped fresh rosemary leaves and minced garlic. Grill, broil or braise the mushrooms. A grill creates the best flavor.

Serve the mushrooms over the polenta.

RISOTTO ALLA MILANESE
Rice with Saffron and Parmigiano

SERVES 4

5	*tablespoons sweet butter, at room temperature*
⅓	*cup finely chopped onion*
1	*cup Arborio rice*
¼	*cup dry white wine*
3½ to 4	*cups hot chicken stock (page 51)*
	Pinch of saffron threads
	Salt and freshly ground black pepper
½	*cup freshly grated Parmigiano*

Melt 4 tablespoons of the butter in a heavy saucepan or casserole. Add the onion and sauté until it is translucent. Add the rice and sauté over low heat for 4 to 5 minutes, stirring constantly.

Add the wine and simmer until it has reduced completely. Add ¼ cup of the stock and stir gently until all the stock has been absorbed. Continue to add the stock ¼ cup at a time, stirring constantly each time, until all the liquid has been absorbed. Once the first cup of stock has been used, add the saffron to the remaining stock. Cook the rice until it is *al dente* (the rice should be creamy, not dry). This will take 15 to 20 minutes.

When the rice is *al dente*, season it with salt and pepper and remove it from the heat. Stir in the remaining tablespoon of butter and the grated Parmigiano. Serve immediately with additional grated Parmigiano.

RISOTTO CON FUNGHI

Rice with Mushrooms and Parmigiano

SERVES 4

1	ounce dried porcini mushrooms
2	cups tepid water
4	tablespoons clarified butter (page 223)
2	tablespoons finely chopped shallots
2	teaspoons finely chopped garlic
1	cup Arborio rice
¾	cup thinly sliced fresh mushrooms
½	teaspoon dried thyme
2	teaspoons finely chopped fresh rosemary leaves
3	fresh sage leaves, finely chopped
¼	cup dry white wine
3	cups, approximately, hot veal stock (page 50) (Chicken stock may be substituted, though the flavor will be milder.)
	Salt and freshly ground black pepper
1	tablespoon butter, at room temperature
½	cup freshly grated Parmigiano

Cover the porcini mushrooms with the tepid water. Weight them down with a plate, if necessary, to keep all the mushrooms submerged. Soak for 1 hour, then remove the mushrooms from the water and rinse them very well to remove all sand and dirt. Strain the soaking liquid through several layers of paper towels and reserve the liquid.

Heat the clarified butter in a heavy saucepan. Add the shallots and garlic and sauté over low heat for 1 minute. Add the rice and sauté for 2 minutes, stirring the rice to coat it with the butter. Add the fresh mushrooms and cook for 2 minutes more. Stir in the thyme, rosemary, sage and wine and let the wine reduce completely.

Heat the stock with ½ cup of the soaking liquid from the porcini. Cut the porcini mushrooms into bite-size pieces.

Add the porcini to the rice. Start adding the stock very slowly (¼ cup at a time). Stir gently until all the stock is absorbed. Continue this process until all the stock is used and the rice is *al dente*, about 15 to 20 minutes. If more stock is needed, use only hot stock.

Remove the pan from the heat and season the rice with salt and pepper. Add the butter and Parmigiano and mix very well. Serve immediately with additional grated Parmigiano, if desired.

RISOTTO CON PISELLI E PROSCIUTTO
Rice with Peas and Prosciutto

SERVES 6

½	cup olive oil
½	large onion, finely chopped
6	thin slices prosciutto (with fat), finely chopped
2	cups Arborio rice
1	cup fresh peas, blanched
2	teaspoons tomato paste
6	cups, approximately, hot chicken stock
	Salt and freshly ground black pepper
½ to 1	cup freshly grated Parmigiano

Heat the olive oil in a heavy-bottomed saucepan. Add the onions and sauté until translucent. Add the prosciutto and stir. Add the rice and sauté for 3 minutes, stirring constantly. Add the peas and sauté for an additional minute.

Dilute the tomato paste in ¼ cup of the stock and add it to the saucepan. Stir gently over low heat until all of the liquid is absorbed. Add the remaining stock ¼ cup at a time, stirring constantly each time until all the stock is absorbed. This will take 15 to 20 minutes.

When the rice is *al dente*, season with salt and pepper and stir in the grated Parmigiano. Serve immediately.

RISOTTO CON FRUTTI DI MARE
Rice with Shrimp, Mussels and Squid

SERVES 6

¼ cup olive oil
4   tablespoons butter, at room temperature
½ medium onion, finely chopped
1   small carrot, finely chopped
½ stalk celery, finely chopped
4   sprigs of fresh parsley, leaves only, finely chopped
1   small bayleaf
4   ounces shrimp, peeled and deveined
4   ounces squid, cleaned and sliced into thin circles
4   ounces mussels, steamed and removed from the shells
3½ cups Arborio rice
¼ cup Cognac
1   cup dry white wine
10 cups, approximately, hot fish stock
2   tablespoons finely chopped fresh basil leaves
    Salt and freshly ground black pepper

Heat the olive oil and 2 tablespoons of the butter together in a heavy-bottomed saucepan. Add the onion, carrot, celery, and bayleaf. Stir and sauté the vegetables until they are tender.

Add the shrimp and squid and sauté until they are opaque. (If the shrimp are large, slice them in half through the back before sautéing.) Remove the shrimp and squid from the pan and set them aside with the cooked mussels. Add the rice to the pan and sauté for about 4 minutes, stirring constantly. Add the cognac and wine and stir. Once these have been absorbed, start to add the fish stock, as for the previous risotto recipes.

When the rice is *al dente*, add the basil, shellfish, salt and pepper, and the remaining butter. Stir to mix and serve immediately.

RISOTTO CON ODORI

Rice with Herbs and Butter

SERVES 6

10 tablespoons butter, at room temperature
1   teaspoon pressed garlic
2   tablespoons finely chopped fresh basil leaves
4   tablespoons finely chopped fresh parsley (leaves only)
2   cups Arborio rice
6   cups, approximately, hot chicken stock
    Salt and freshly ground black pepper
6   tablespoons freshly grated Pecorino romano

Melt 6 tablespoons of the butter in a heavy-bottomed saucepan. Add the garlic, basil, and parsley and sauté over low heat for one minute.

Add the rice to the pan and sauté for 4 minutes, stirring constantly. Add the stock as for the previous risotto recipes.

When the rice is *al dente*, stir in the remaining butter, salt and pepper, and 3 tablespoons of the grated cheese. Stir to mix. Serve immediately with the remaining cheese sprinkled on top.

RISOTTO CON CARCIOFI A PEPERONI
Rice with Artichoke Hearts and Sweet Red Peppers
SERVES 6

6	artichoke hearts
1	lemon
4	tablespoons butter
1	small onion, finely chopped
1	garlic clove, finely chopped
2	tablespoons finely chopped fresh parsley (leaves only)
6	thin slices prosciutto (with fat), finely chopped
2	cups Arborio rice
1	cup dry white wine
6	cups, approximately, hot chicken stock
2	roasted sweet red peppers, peeled, seeded and coarsely chopped
	Salt and freshly ground black pepper
½	cup freshly grated Parmigiano

Slice the artichoke hearts into ¼-inch-thick wedges. Place them in a bowl with enough water to cover and the juice of the lemon added. Let stand until ready to use.

Melt the butter in a heavy-bottomed saucepan. Add the onion and garlic and sauté until the onion is translucent. Drain the artichokes and pat them dry with paper towels. Add them to the pan along with the prosciutto and parsley. Lower the heat and sauté for 2 minutes, stirring constantly. Add the rice and sauté for 2 minutes, stirring constantly. Add the wine and stir until it is absorbed.

Add the chicken stock as for the previous risotto recipes.

When the rice is *al dente*, add the roasted peppers, salt and pepper and Parmigiano. Stir gently to mix and serve immediately.

PESCI E FRUTTI DI MARE

Fish and Shellfish

One afternoon in the summer of 1958 Ciro and Sal were cleaning a few good-sized striped bass in the garden of the restaurant. A French couple walked by and asked if the fish would be on the menu. "Of course," was the answer. That evening the couple returned and ordered the bass. They enjoyed it so much that they returned the next three nights and sampled the rest of the fish dishes. All received high praises. At the time, the man told Ciro that he was a maitre d' on an ocean liner.

Two years later, returning from a trip to Europe on the USS Independence, Ciro met the Frenchman, Charles Masson, who was maitre d' in first class. Masson made certain that Ciro would receive the best treatment and invited Ciro up to his office. There on the wall was a framed copy of the CIRO & SAL's menu.

In 1982, Charles Masson and his wife opened Manhattan's LA GRENOUILLE restaurant.

◆———◆

PESCE ALLA GIOSUE

Poached Fish and Clams with White Wine and Herbs

SERVES 4

4	tablespoons olive oil
3	garlic cloves, finely chopped
5	shallots, finely chopped
4	1¼-inch-thick striped bass steaks
12	littleneck clams
1¼	cups dry white wine
¾	cup fish stock (page 52)
1¼	teaspoons dried basil or chopped fresh basil leaves
	Pinch of hot red pepper flakes
	Pinch of dried rosemary or chopped fresh rosemary leaves
2	tablespoons chopped fresh chives
	Salt and freshly ground black pepper

Heat the oil in a skillet. Add the garlic and shallots and sauté until they are golden.

Add the fish and all the remaining ingredients. Cover the pan and poach the fish for about 10 minutes, or until it is done.

Transfer the fish to a warm serving dish. Cook the sauce over high heat to reduce it slightly, then pour over the fish.

NOTE: This sauce is excellent served over spaghetti or linguine. Simply cook the pasta while the fish is poaching. Pour half of the sauce over the fish steaks and the remainder over the pasta.

SPIGOLA ALLA PROCIDANA

Striped Bass Broiled with Red Wine Vinegar and Mint

SERVES 4

8	tablespoons olive oil
½	cup red wine vinegar
½	cup dry white wine
3	teaspoons dried basil
1	teaspoon dried oregano
	Salt and freshly ground pepper
4	10-ounce striped bass steaks
8	whole fresh mint leaves

Preheat the broiler.

Combine the first 6 ingredients in a shallow, ovenproof pan. Add the fish to the pan, then lay 2 mint leaves on each steak.

Broil the bass on both sides until it is done. Transfer the steaks to a warm serving dish and pour the sauce over them. Garnish with additional fresh mint sprigs.

PESCE AL FORNO

Whole Bluefish Baked with Garlic, Rosemary and Basil

SERVES 12 TO 16

1	8-pound whole bluefish
	Salt and freshly ground black pepper
8	sprigs fresh rosemary
3	bunches fresh basil
3	cups extra virgin olive oil
2	heads garlic, finely chopped
1	small bunch fresh parsley, finely chopped

Preheat the oven to 375 degrees.

Scale and gut the fish. Then wash it thoroughly, inside and out, in cold water. Rub salt and pepper into the cavity, and stuff with 3 rosemary sprigs and 1 bunch of basil.

Pour the olive oil into a baking pan large enough to hold the fish. Add the garlic, parsley, salt and pepper. Chop the remaining basil and add it to the oil. Stir well. Lay the fish on the oil and roll it around once to coat it with the seasoned oil. Lay the 5 remaining rosemary sprigs over the fish. Cover the pan with aluminum foil and bake for 40 to 45 minutes.

To serve, lift the skin off the top side of the fish. Cut down to the bone, making rectangular portions. Lift each portion off the bones with a narrow spatula. Spoon a little of the oil and herbs from the pan over each portion. Turn the fish over and repeat the process to serve from the other side.

PESCE ALLA SARDENESE

Fish Sautéed with Green Pepper and Coriander

SERVES 4

2	tablespoons olive oil
1	onion, sliced into thin rounds
1	sweet green pepper, seeded and sliced very thin
4	8-ounce haddock, halibut, flounder or bass fillets
	Juice of 1 lime
½	cup dry white wine
4	tomatoes, peeled, seeded and chopped
2	teaspoons finely chopped fresh parsley leaves
2	teaspoons chopped fresh coriander leaves
	Salt and freshly ground black pepper

Heat the oil in a large skillet. Add the onion and sauté for 5 minutes. Add the green pepper and sauté for 3 to 4 minutes. Remove the vegetables from the pan and set them aside.

Raise the heat and add the fish to the pan. Sauté for several minutes on each side (the cooking time will depend on the thickness of the fish). Return the vegetables to the pan and add the remaining ingredients; reduce for 1 minute.

Transfer the fish to warm serving plates and garnish with the vegetables and some of the sauce. Serve immediately.

HALIBUT CON SALSA VERDE
Broiled Halibut with Green Suace

SERVES 4

¼ cup fresh bread crumbs made from crustless bread
2 tablespoons red wine vinegar
¼ cup extra virgin olive oil
   Juice of ½ lemon
½ cup fresh basil leaves
½ cup fresh parsley leaves
10 anchovy fillets, rinsed and dried
2 hard-boiled large egg yolks
   Salt and freshly ground black pepper
4 10-ounce halibut skinless fillets
1 large garlic clove, sliced in half
   Juice of 1 lemon
   Coarsely ground black pepper
¼ cup extra virgin olive oil
   Salt

Preheat the broiler.

Prepare the Salsa Verde. Soak the bread crumbs in the wine vinegar. Squeeze all the excess vinegar out of the bread crumbs and then combine them with the next 7 ingredients in a food processor or blender and blend until smooth.

Rub the halibut fillets with the garlic, lemon juice and coarsely ground black pepper. (Reserve some of the lemon juice.) Place the fillets in an ovenproof dish. Sprinkle them with the remaining lemon juice, olive oil and salt. Broil until done, turning the fillets once. Just before the fillets are done, place 2 tablespoons of the Salsa Verde on each fillet. Return them to the broiler for a moment and serve immediately.

SOGLIOLA SEMPLICE

Sole Sautéed with Shallots and Scallions

SERVES 4

⅓   cup olive oil
3   garlic cloves, finely chopped
4   shallots, finely chopped
6   scallions, white and green parts, sliced on the diagonal
4   10-ounce sole or flounder fillets
1½ cups thinly sliced fresh mushrooms
2   tablespoons dry vermouth
    Juice of 1 lemon
2   teaspoons finely chopped fresh parsley
    Salt and freshly ground black pepper
    Lemon wedges and parsley sprigs for garnish

Heat the oil in a skillet. Add the garlic, shallots and scallions and sauté for 5 minutes, or until the shallots and scallions are translucent. Be careful not to burn the garlic.

Add all the remaining ingredients, except the lemon wedges and parsley sprigs, and cook the fillets over medium heat until they are opaque.

Transfer the fillets to a warm serving dish and pour the vegetables and sauce over them. Garnish with the lemon wedges and parsley sprigs.

SOGLIOLA DI NOZZE

Poached Sole with Tarragon and Sour Cream Sauce

SERVES 4

⅓   cup clarified butter (page 223)
½   cup dry white wine
     Juice of 1 lmeon
4   10-ounce sole or flounder fillets
1   teaspoon chopped fresh tarragon leaves
     Salt and freshly ground black pepper
1   cup sour cream, at room temperature, and whipped to a more
         liquid consistency
3   tablespoons chopped fresh chives

Heat the butter in a skillet. Add the wine, lemon juice, fish and tarragon. Season with a little salt and pepper. Cover the pan and poach the fish over low heat just until the fish becomes opaque.

Transfer the fish to a warm serving dish. Return the liquid in the skillet to a boil and whisk in the sour cream and chives. If necessary, add more salt and pepper. Pour the sauce over the fillets and serve immediately.

SOGLIOLA ALLA PRIMAVERA

Sautéed Sole with Vegetable Purée

SERVES 4

2   cups peeled and seeded ripe tomatoes
½   cup chopped carrots
½   cup chopped zucchini
2   shallots, peeled
⅓   cup clarified butter (page 223)
1   bay leaf
2   pounds sole or flounder fillets
½   cup dry white wine
⅓   cup fish stock (page 52)
½   teaspoon dried thyme or chopped fresh thyme leaves
     Salt and freshly ground black pepper
2   scallions, thinly sliced on the diagonal

Combine the tomatoes, carrot, zucchini and shallots in a food processor and process until finely chopped.

Heat half the butter in a skillet and add the chopped vegetables and bay leaf. Cook over low heat for 12 minutes. Press the vegetables through a coarse sieve, then set them aside.

In the same skillet, heat the remaining butter. Add the fish, wine, stock, thyme, salt and pepper. Cover and poach the fish just until it becomes opaque.

Transfer the fish to a warm serving dish. Add the vegetables to the skillet and stir to mix. Cook for 2 minutes to reduce the sauce. Pour the sauce over the fish and garnish with the scallions.

BRODETTO DI PESCE

Fish Stew with Tomatoes and Herbs

SERVES 4

¼   cup olive oil
2   garlic cloves, finely chopped
4   shallots, finely chopped
4   1¼-inch-thick cod, bass or bluefish steaks
12   littleneck clams, washed
¼   cup dry red wine
¼   cup dry white wine
1½   cups Marinara Sauce (page 87)
1   tablespoon chopped fresh basil leaves
1   bay leaf
2   teaspoons finely chopped fresh parsley leaves
     Salt and freshly ground black pepper
     Chopped fresh parsley or basil leaves for garnish

Heat the oil in a large skillet. Add the garlic and shallots and
sauté until they are golden.

Add the fish, clams, red and white wines. Cover the pan and
bring to a boil, then lower the heat and simmer for 3 minutes. Add the
remaining ingredients, cover the pan again and simmer until done,
about 10 minutes.

Transfer the fish to a warm serving platter and arrange the clams
around it. Pour the sauce over the fish and clams and garnish with
chopped fresh parsley or basil leaves.

NOTE: The brodetto is excellent served with spaghetti that has been
sauced with some of the brodetto. Garlic croutons are also an excellent accompaniment. (Arrange the croutons around the fish and pour
sauce over them as well.)

To make the croutons, slice a thin loaf of french bread on the
diagonal (the slices should be ¼-inch-thick). Drizzle extra virgin olive
oil over each slice and sprinkle with salt. Bake in a 400 degree oven
until golden. Rub both sides of each slice with a split clove of garlic.
Serve immediately.

PESCE MISTO

Mixed Fish Poached with Tomatoes and Pernod

SERVES 4 TO 6

1	cup olive oil
2	garlic cloves, finely chopped
1	medium-size onion, finely chopped
2	celery stalks, finely chopped
1	cup fish stock (page 52)
1	cup dry white wine
¼	cup chopped fresh tarragon leaves
¼	cup fennel seeds, crushed
¼	teaspoon ground turmeric
⅛	teaspoon freshly ground black pepper
4	ripe tomatoes, peeled, seeded and chopped
1	tablespoon Pernod
½	cup finely chopped fresh parsley leaves
16	mussels, scrubbed and debearded
12	littleneck clams, washed
8	shrimp, shelled and deveined
1	pound haddock or bluefish
6	soft-shelled crabs, cleaned and dredged in flour

Preheat the oven to 400 degrees.

Heat half of the oil in a deep skillet. Add the garlic, onion and celery and sauté for 5 minutes. Add the stock, wine, tarragon, fennel, turmeric and black pepper. Simmer for 10 minutes and then add the tomatoes, parsley and Pernod. Simmer for another 5 minutes.

Add the mussels and clams to the pan, cover and cook over moderate to high heat until they have opened. Remove the shellfish from the pan and set aside.

To the same skillet add the fish and shrimp. Leave only enough sauce in the pan to poach the fish. (Reserve the extra sauce.) Cover the pan and poach the fish over low heat just until they are cooked.

Heat the remaining oil in another skillet and sauté the soft-shelled crabs for about 3 minutes on each side, or until brown.

Combine all the seafood except the crabs in a large ovenproof serving dish. Pour a generous amount of the sauce over the seafood but do not make it a soup. Place the crabs on top and cover the dish with aluminum foil. Bake until all the ingredients are well heated.

Some days friends would come by the restaurant with fish or other foods to make dinner for the "gang." One day artist and friend Edward Giobbi prepared a dish with fish, shellfish and chicken. Everyone loved it. It was 1957, the year that the Chrysler Museum opened in Provincetown, and Walter Chrysler was having a dinner party at the restaurant for fifty people. The guests included Hudson Walker, the founder of the Fine Arts Work Center, and the artist Seong Moy. With Eddie's help, Ciro and Sal prepared the Cacciucco for all fifty people. It was so well received by the guests that they decided to keep it on the menu.

Edward Giobbi is a successful artist and has published two cookbooks since his one-night stint at CIRO's, and his recipes have been featured frequently by Craig Claiborne in The New York Times.

◆————————◆

CACCIUCCO ALLA LIVORNESE
Fish Stew with Capers and Fresh Herbs

SERVES 4

1	1½-pound chicken, cut into 10 or 12 pieces
½	cup olive oil
3	garlic cloves, peeled
¼	cup red wine vinegar
¼	cup dry white wine
	Salt and freshly ground black pepper
3	cups Marinara Sauce (page 87)
1	tablespoon capers, rinsed and drained
1	tablespoon chopped fresh basil leaves
1	teaspoon chopped fresh rosemary leaves
2	tablespoons finely chopped fresh parsley leaves
1	1¾-pounds lobster
8	littleneck clams, washed
12	mussels, washed and debearded
1	pound haddock or cod
8	shrimp, shelled and deveined
2	squid, cleaned and sliced into ¼-inch rings

Preheat the oven to 400 degrees.

Heat the oil in a skillet. Add the chicken and the garlic and brown the chicken on both sides. Lower the heat and add the vinegar, wine, salt and pepper. Cook until the chicken is almost done then remove and set aside. Discard the garlic.

Add the Marinara sauce, capers, basil, rosemary and 1 tablespoon of the parsley to the skillet. Simmer for 5 minutes.

Transfer the sauce to a roasting pan and add the lobster, clams and mussels to the pan. Place the pan over two burners on top of the stove. Cover the pan and cook for 15 minutes.

Place the fish, shrimp and squid in another skillet. Add 1 cup of the sauce from the lobster pan. Cover the skillet and cook over medium heat, being careful not to overcook. The fish and shellfish should be slightly underdone.

Combine the chicken, fish, shrimp and squid in the roasting pan with the lobster, clams and mussels. Cover the pan with aluminum foil and bake for 10 minutes.

Remove the pan from the oven. Crack the lobster claws and split the tail. Arrange the remaining seafood and chicken on a large serving dish. Arrange the lobster pieces on top and pour about 2 cups of the sauce over all. Sprinkle the remaining tablespoon of parsley on top.

BACCALÀ SEMPLICE
Simple Salt Cod

SERVES 6

2	pounds salt cod
3	garlic cloves, peeled
2	parsley sprigs
½	cup extra virgin olive oil
	Freshly ground black pepper

Soak the salt cod in abundant cold water for 24 hours, changing the water often. Remove it from the water and rinse it with fresh cold water. Remove the skin and trim away any excess fat or bones. Divide the fish into 6 portions.

Put the cod in a large casserole. Add the garlic, parsley and 3 tablespoons of the olive oil. Cover the cod with cold water and bring to a boil, then lower the heat and simmer for 20 minutes.

Transfer the cod to warm serving plates. Drizzle the cod with a generous amount of olive oil and sprinkle with pepper.

PESCE IN UMIDO

Fish Stewed with Anchovies, Capers and Fresh Herbs

SERVES 4

¼	cup olive oil
3	garlic cloves, finely chopped
4	anchovy fillets, rinsed, dried and chopped
4	10-ounce bluefish or cod steaks
2	tablespoons dry red wine
1	cup dry white wine
1	tablespoon red wine vinegar
1	tablespoon capers, rinsed and drained
1	tablespoon chopped fresh basil leaves
½	teaspoon dried oregano
½	teaspoon chopped fresh rosemary leaves
2	teaspoons finely chopped fresh parsley leaves
¼	teaspoon hot red pepper flakes
4	slices ripe tomato
1½	cups Marinara Sauce (page 87)
	Parsley sprigs for garnish

Heat the oil in a large skillet. Add the garlic and anchovies and sauté until the garlic is golden and the anchovies have dissolved (mash them with a fork).

Add all the remaining ingredients, except the Marinara sauce, to the pan. The tomato slices should be placed on the fish steaks. Cover the pan and cook the fish over low heat for 3 minutes.

Add the Marinara sauce to the pan and simmer until the fish is done, about 8 minutes.

Transfer to a warm serving dish and garnish with the parsley sprigs.

BACCALÀ IN UMIDO ALLA GENOVINA

Genovina's Stewed Salt Cod with Potatoes

SERVES 6

2   pounds salt cod
¼   cup olive oil
1   onion, finely chopped
1   garlic clove, finely chopped
2   pounds white potatoes, peeled and cut into ¼-inch wedges
4   plum tomatoes, peeled, seeded and chopped
2   parsley sprigs
     Freshly ground black pepper

Soak the salt cod in abundant cold water for 24 hours, changing the water often. Remove it from the water and rinse it in cold water. Remove the skin and trim away any excess fat or bones. Cut into pieces approximately 2 × 1 inch.

Heat the olive oil in a heavy casserole. Add the onions and garlic and sauté until the onion is translucent. Add the potatoes, lower the heat and cook for 10 minutes.

Add the salt cod, tomatoes, parsley and pepper. Stir gently. If the stew seems too dry, add a little white wine or water. Cover the pot and cook slowly for 20 minutes.

CONCHIGLIE E ANIMELLE

Scallops and Sweetbreads Sautéed with Fresh Morels and Madeira

SERVES 4

1	pound sweetbreads
1	celery stalk, chopped
1	onion, chopped
½	carrot, chopped
2	tablespoons red wine vinegar
	Salt and freshly ground black pepper
2	tablespoons clarified butter (page 223)
1	tablespoon finely chopped shallots
1	pound sea scallops
¼	cup dry Madeira
½	pound fresh morels (Sliced fresh mushrooms may be substituted.)
2 to 4	tablespoons sweet butter, softened

Remove the fat and tubes from the sweetbreads. Cover them with cold water to which a little salt has been added. Soak for 1 to 2 hours, then drain.

Put the sweetbreads in a saucepan. Cover with cold water and add the celery, onion, carrot, vinegar, salt and pepper. Bring to a boil, then lower the heat and simmer for 5 minutes. Drain and cool under cold running water. Cut the sweetbreads into ¼-inch-thick slices, removing any membranes or connective tissue.

Heat the butter in a large skillet. Add the shallots and sauté for 1 minute (do not burn). Add the scallops and sauté for 2 minutes, then add the mushrooms and sauté for another 2 minutes. Add the sweetbreads and stir gently. Add the Madeira and move the pan in quick circular motions to facilitate the reduction of the wine, about 1 to 2 minutes.

Remove the scallops and sweetbreads to a warm serving dish.

Whisk the butter quickly into the sauce and season with salt and pepper. Pour the sauce over the scallops and sweetbreads. Serve immediately.

CONCHIGLIE AL GIMINGNANO

Scallops Broiled with Mushrooms and Madeira

SERVES 4

1½ pounds sea or bay scallops
1   cup thinly sliced fresh mushrooms
½   cup olive oil
½   cup Madeira
     Juice of ½ lemon
2   garlic cloves, pressed
     Salt and freshly ground black pepper

Preheat the broiler.

In a shallow, ovenproof pan combine the scallops, mushrooms, oil, wine, lemon juice, garlic, salt and pepper.

Place the pan under the broiler (it should be 2 inches from the heat source) and cook for 5 to 6 minutes, turning the scallops once. Be careful not to overcook them.

Transfer the scallops to a warm serving dish and pour the sauce over them. Serve immediately.

ZUPPA DI VONGOLE

Clams Cooked with Wine and Herbs

SERVES 4

½   cup olive oil
4   garlic cloves, finely chopped
8   shallots, finely chopped
½   cup dry red wine
½   cup dry white wine
2   tablespoons dried basil or chopped fresh basil leaves
1   teaspoon hot red pepper flakes
2   tablespoons finely chopped fresh parsley leaves
48   littleneck clams, washed
2   cups Marinara Sauce (page 87)

Heat the oil in a large deep saucepan or rondo. Add the garlic and shallots and sauté until they are golden. Add all the remaining ingredients, cover the pan and cook over moderate heat until all the clams have opened.

Arrange the clams in a serving bowl and pour the sauce over them.

◆————————◆

"*When I first came to Provincetown in 1955, I noticed that the rocks in the bay were loaded with mussels. I was amazed to find that no one picked them, but soon found out that most of the townspeople thought of them as a type of barnacle. In South Philadelphia where I was born, the Italian bars served the mussels steamed with olive oil, garlic and hot pepper seeds.*

"That summer in Provincetown I often made them and turned many people on to them. I told Ciro to put them on the menu, but he insisted that no one would order them. He was probably right. The Italians, Spaniards, French and Armenians ate them, but not one seafood restaurant in this country served them. It was seven years before Ciro put mussels on the menu, and his was one of the first restaurants to do so."

—AL DiLAURO

COZZE AL COZZI

Mussels Poached in White Wine and Herbs

SERVES 4

2	tablespoons olive oil
2	garlic cloves, finely chopped
¼	cup dry white wine
1	teaspoon dried basil or chopped fresh basil leaves
¼	teaspoon dried oregano
¼	teaspoon hot red pepper flakes
1	tablespoon finely chopped fresh parsley leaves
	Salt and freshly ground black pepper
40	mussels, scrubbed and debearded

Heat the olive oil in a large saucepan. Add the garlic and sauté until it is golden. Add the remaining ingredients, cover the pan and simmer gently until all the mussels have opened, about 7 minutes.

Arrange the mussels on a large serving dish or in a large bowl and pour the sauce over them. Serve immediately.

SCAMPI ALLA GRIGLIA

Shrimp Broiled with Scallions and Butter

SERVES 4

1⅓ cups clarified butter (page 223)
⅔   cup olive oil
2   garlic cloves, peeled
2   small onions, chopped
     Juice of 1 lemon
     Salt and freshly ground black pepper
6   scallions, white and green parts, thinly sliced on the diagonal
28   large shrimp, shelled and deveined.

Preheat the broiler.

Combine the butter, oil, garlic, onion, lemon juice, salt and pepper in a bowl and blend thoroughly with a whisk.

Put the shrimp in a shallow ovenproof pan and sprinkle the scallions over them. Pour the butter and oil mixture over the shrimp. Put the pan under the broiler (3 inches from the heat source) and broil for about 3 minutes on each side.

Transfer the shrimp to a warm serving dish and pour the sauce over them.

ARAGOSTA PICCANTE AL CIRO
Lobster with Piquant Sauce

SERVES 4

2	2-pound live lobsters
¼	cup olive oil
¾	cup coarsely chopped shallots
8	anchovy fillets, rinsed and chopped
4	garlic cloves, finely chopped
½	cup dry red wine
1	cup fish stock (page 52)
½	cup Dijon mustard
2	tablespoons tomato paste
1	teaspoon chopped fresh rosemary leaves
1	teaspoon chopped fresh sage leaves
	Coarsely ground black pepper
4	tablespoons red wine vinegar
¼	cup finely chopped fresh parsley leaves

Prepare the lobsters: Pierce them through the head to kill them; crack the claws, legs and knuckles and split the tails.

Heat the oil in a large pan and sauté the lobster pieces over high heat for 10 minutes. Add the shallots, anchovies, garlic, wine and stock. Lower the heat and simmer for 10 minutes.

Stir in the mustard, tomato paste, rosemary, sage and black pepper. Cover and cook for 5 minutes more. Add the vinegar and half of the parsley.

Remove the lobster and cook the sauce over low heat for 20 minutes.

Using lobster shears cut away the top half of the claws. Cut the undersides of the tails and spread them open. Do the same with the knuckles. Leave all the lobster meat in the shells. Arrange the lobster, reproducing its true shape, on a warm platter. Place in a warm (250-degree) oven, if necessary, until the sauce is ready.

Spoon the sauce over the lobster and sprinkle with the remaining parsley.

MOLECHE DI SAN GENNARO

Soft-Shell Crabs Sautéed
with White Wine and Lemon

SERVES 4

16   *soft-shelled crabs*
½   *cup all-purpose flour*
     Salt and freshly ground black pepper
1   *cup clarified butter (page 223)*
4   *garlic cloves, finely chopped*
6   *shallots, finely chopped*
     Juice of ½ lemon
½   *cup dry white wine*
3   *tablespoons finely chopped fresh parsley leaves*
8   *thin lemon slices for garnish*

Clean the crabs: Pierce them between the eyes with a knife, lift the pointed ends of the shells and scrape out the spongy portion between the shell and the body. Put the crabs on their backs and cut off the flaps on the bottom sides. Wash them thoroughly in cold water and dry completely.

Combine the flour with a little salt and pepper in a shallow pan. Dredge the crabs in the flour and shake off any excess.

Heat the butter in a large skillet and sauté the crabs until they are brown and crisp on one side. Turn them over and add the garlic and shallots to the pan. Sauté until the crabs are brown and crisp on the second side, being careful not to burn the garlic and shallots.

Transfer the crabs to a warm serving plate. Add the lemon juice, wine and parsley to the pan and cook over high heat for about 2 minutes. Pour the sauce over the crabs and garnish with the lemon slices.

PESCE ADRIATICO

Poached Fish and Shellfish with Caper-Butter Sauce

SERVES 4

4   7-ounce haddock or fillets of halibut steaks
24   mussels, washed and debearded
12   shrimp, shelled and deveined
2   tablespoons capers, rinsed and drained
½   cup dry white wine
     Generous splash of red wine vinegar
2   teaspoons chopped fresh rosemary leaves
1   teaspoon dried thyme
     Salt and freshly ground black pepper
10   tablespoons butter, softened

Place all the ingredients, except 8 tablespoons of the butter, into a large saucepan (if necessary, use 2 pans). Cover the pan and bring to a boil. Lower the heat and simmer until the mussels have opened and the fish is flaky.

Remove the fish and shellfish to a warm serving platter. Add the butter to the pan and whisk it rapidly into the sauce. Season with more salt and pepper. Pour the sauce over the fish and shellfish and serve immediately.

POLLO

Chicken

A *young woman began her love affair with food after eating at* CIRO & SAL'S *and was inspired to open her own restaurant.* ALICE'S RESTAURANT *went on to garner its own special fame, and although Alice May Brock's place is closed now, she continues to get anything she wants at* CIRO & SAL'S.

ODE TO CIRO AND SAL

There are certain moments, certain places, that stick in your mind, that become guidelines, the ultimate experience that all others are compared with, and, of course, fall short of.

I spent my first twelve summers in Provincetown on Cape Cod. My father worked with a fellow up there named Peter Hunt who owned a whole alleyway of shops. One summer, a little coffee and sandwich place—an outdoor café—appeared in the alley. My only interest in it was that my "boyfriend's" mother worked there. It was owned by two artists, Ciro Cozzi and Sal Del Deo. Shortly after they opened up, I stopped going to Provincetown. I was a teenager and wanted to stay in Brooklyn with the guys and go to Coney Island.

I went back to Provincetown when I was about eighteen. My father gave me fifty dollars to rent a bike, buy flipper dough and eat at Ciro and Sal's on Wednesday night. The special was "Cacciucco Livornese"— whole lobster, chicken, cherrystone clams, mussels and other varieties of seafood, baked in a light sauce of tomato, wine and herbs, en casserole. Being a dutiful daughter and mostly because my father knew what was good, I went—down the old Peter Hunt Alley, into a court-yard, down a few stone steps, into a tiny room sparkling with candles, and filled with the most wonderful smells my nose had ever encoun-tered. I sat down at a tiny table on a very uncomfortable nail keg and

119

ordered the special. What happened after that is history. I've never forgotten that meal. It was one of the first I had had the pleasure of eating alone and uninterrupted. I closed my eyes, I rocked in ecstasy; I sucked on mussel shells and rolled rice and sauce around in my mouth. It was heaven. I remember discussing the food with my sister, who had done the same thing. We were in awe.

Then a few more years passed. I opened and closed my first restaurant. And one April evening I found myself back in Province-town. I went to Ciro's. It was bigger, and they had a liquor license, but the smells were the same—wonderful. I went upstairs and sat alone in a corner. I ordered a bottle of wine, a pile of steamed mussels and an order of fried zucchini. Life once again took on new dimensions. I asked the waiter—Dennis was his name—how the veal was. "We are famous for our veal." Great! I ordered another bottle of wine, and "Veal Piccata—scallops of veal with mushrooms, lemon and cream." Dennis thought it was too much. "Don't worry, sweetheart, I can handle it."

After dinner I was in seventh heaven, a bit crocked, and I sent a note down to the kitchen. I don't remember now the exact wording, but it was a love note. I wrote that I had eaten there when I was younger, and I had never forgotten it. Since then I had opened a restaurant myself and was inspired by Ciro and Sal's. I signed it "Alice of Alice's Restaurant," something I had never done before.

Dennis came back up with my brandy, followed by Ciro and everybody else who worked there. There was lots of brandy and laughing and hugging and smiling and kissing as Ciro and I talked about veal with such zeal that we finally lunged at each other across the table, screaming ravioli, cannelloni and spinach noodles, and zuppa di pesce. All in all, it was a wonderful meeting.

Thank you, Ciro and Sal's.

(Reprinted from *My Life as a Restaurant* by Alice May Brock.)

POLLO ARROSTO CON PATATE E ROSMARINO

Roast Chicken with Potatoes and Rosemary

SERVES 4

1   3-pound chicken, cut into quarters, washed and trimmed of
      excess fat
1   garlic clove, cut in half
     Salt and freshly ground black pepper
1   cup olive oil
1   tablespoon chopped fresh rosemary leaves
4   Idaho potatoes, washed and dried

Preheat the oven to 375 degrees.

Rub the chicken pieces on all sides with the garlic, salt, pepper and some of the olive oil. Sprinkle with 2 teaspoons of the rosemary.

Rub some of the oil over the bottom of a large roasting pan. Arrange the chicken quarters, skin side up, in the center of the pan.

Slice the potatoes into ½-inch wedges. Put the potatoes in a bowl and pour the remaining oil over them. Toss well to coat the potatoes completely with the oil. Arrange the potatoes around the chicken. They should be arranged, skin side down, one next to the other, not overlapping. Sprinkle the potatoes with salt, pepper and the remaining rosemary.

Bake uncovered for 1 hour or until the chicken is done. Baste the chicken frequently with its own juices. When done, the potatoes will be crispy outside and fluffy inside.

POLLO ALLA BOLOGNESE

Roasted Chicken with a Brandy-Cream Sauce

SERVES 4 TO 6

1	3-pound chicken, cut into 4 or 6 pieces
¼	cup olive oil
1	garlic glove, cut in half
1	teaspoon dried tarragon or chopped fresh tarragon leaves
	Salt and freshly ground black pepper
¾	cup dry white wine
¼	cup dry sherry
¼	cup brandy
6	tablespoons butter
1	cup thinly sliced fresh mushrooms
1	carrot, finely chopped
1	celery stalk, finely chopped
1	medium-size onion, finely chopped
½	teaspoon dried thyme
1	garlic clove, finely chopped
½	cup chicken stock (page 51)
½	cup heavy cream

Preheat the oven to 350 degrees. Coat the bottom of a roasting pan with half the oil.

Rub the chicken pieces with the remaining oil and the garlic halves, then sprinkle each piece with the tarragon, salt and pepper. Arrange the chicken, skin side up, in the baking pan. Bake uncovered for 45 minutes or until done. Baste the chicken with ½ cup of the white wine, ¼ cup sherry and 3 tablespoons of the brandy throughout the baking period. Drain the fat from the pan, reserving the chicken juices.

While the chicken is cooking prepare the vegetables.

Heat 3 tablespoons of the butter in a skillet and sauté the mushrooms until they are tender. Season them with salt and pepper, then remove the mushrooms to a warm plate and cover to keep them warm.

In the same pan, heat the remaining 3 tablespoons of butter and sauté the carrot, celery and onion until they are tender. Add the thyme, salt and pepper to taste. Cover and set aside.

Prepare the sauce. Pour the remaining wine and brandy into a hot skillet, bring to a boil and cook off the alcohol. Add the chopped garlic, stock, salt and pepper to taste, and simmer for 3 minutes. Add the juices from the baking pan (about ¼ cup), and the heavy cream and simmer for 5 minutes.

Arrange the chicken pieces on a warm serving platter. Arrange the carrot, celery, and onion mixture around the chicken. Sprinkle the mushrooms over the chicken. Pour the sauce over all and serve immediately.

POLLO ALL'ARRABBIATO
Roast Chicken with Red Pepper

SERVES 4 TO 8

2	2-pound chickens, cut into quarters
½	cup olive oil
1	garlic clove, cut in half
1¼	teaspoons cayenne pepper
	Salt and freshly ground black pepper
½	cup dry white wine
8 to 10	fresh artichoke hearts
¼	of a fresh lemon
4	tablespoons butter
1½	cups thinly sliced fresh mushrooms
1	cup Espagnole Sauce (page 195)
8	½-inch slices roasted sweet red peppers

Preheat the oven to 375 degrees. Coat the bottom of a roasting pan with half of the oil.

Rub the chicken with the remaining oil and the garlic halves, then sprinkle each piece with ⅛ teaspoon of the cayenne pepper and some salt and black pepper. Arrange the chicken in the pan and bake uncovered for 50 minutes, or until done. Baste the chicken with the white wine throughout the baking period. Strain the fat from the pan and reserve the juices.

While the chicken is cooking, blanch the artichokes in boiling water with the lemon until they are tender, then drain. Heat the butter in a skillet and sauté the mushrooms until tender, add the artichoke hearts, salt and pepper and mix well. Cover and set aside.

Prepare the sauce. Heat the Espagnole Sauce in a saucepan. Add the juices from the chicken, the remaining ¼ teaspoon of cayenne pepper, salt and pepper. Simmer for 5 minutes.

Stir ¼ cup of the sauce into the pan with the artichokes and mushrooms. Simmer, stirring, for 5 minutes.

Briefly heat the peppers in a separate pan.

Arrange the chicken on a warm serving platter. Top the pieces with the roasted red pepper slices. Arrange the artichoke mixture around the chicken and pour the sauce over all.

POLLO ALLA RAVINELLA

Roast Chicken with Baby Onions and Carrots in Brown Sauce

SERVES 4 TO 8

2	2-pound chickens, cut into quarters
¼	cup olive oil
1	garlic clove, cut in half
1½	tablespoons dried rosemary, crushed
	Salt and freshly ground black pepper
⅔	cup dry white wine
⅔	cup Espagnole Sauce (page 195)
¼	cup chicken stock (page 51)
1	tablespoon red wine vinegar
½	teaspoon dry mustard
3 to 4	tablespoons butter
1½	cup fresh mushrooms cut into halves
3	carrots, cut into julienne
1½	cups peeled pearl onions

Preheat the oven to 375 degrees. Coat the bottom of a baking pan with half of the oil.

Rub the chicken pieces with the remaining oil and the garlic halves, then sprinkle the rosemary and salt and pepper over each piece. Arrange the chicken, skin side up, in the pan and bake uncovered for about 50 minutes, or until done. Baste the chicken with the white wine throughout the baking period.

While the chicken is cooking prepare the sauce and vegetables. Combine the Espagnole Sauce, stock, vinegar, dry mustard, salt and pepper in a saucepan. Bring to a boil and simmer for 5 minutes.

Melt the butter in a skillet and sauté the mushrooms until they are tender.

Blanch the carrots and pearl onions in salted boiling water. Drain and add to the mushrooms. Stir to mix. Set aside.

After the chicken has cooked for 40 minutes, baste it with ¼ cup of the sauce. When the chicken is done, degrease the pan juices and strain them into the remaining sauce. Simmer for 3 minutes. .

Heat the vegetables over moderate heat for 2 to 3 minutes.

Arrange the chicken on a warm serving platter and arrange the vegetables around it. Pour the sauce over the chicken and vegetables and serve immediately.

PETTO DI POLLO CON BROCCOLI

Stuffed Chicken Breast with Broccoli and Pesto-Cream Sauce

SERVES 4

2   cups broccoli flowerets, blanched
1   cup chopped fresh mushrooms
½   cup chopped mozzarella
¼   cup freshly grated Parmigiano
½   cup bread crumbs
1   teaspoon dried rosemary or chopped fresh rosemary leaves
4   large chicken breasts, boned but not skinned
4   teaspoons plus 2 tablespoons Pesto (page 89)
     Freshly ground black pepper, and salt
4   thin slices of prosciutto
⅓   cup clarified butter (page 223)
¼   cup dry white wine
¼   cup chicken stock (page 51)
1   cup light cream
2   tablespoons dry sherry

In a food processor, blend together the broccoli, mushrooms, mozzarella, Parmigiano, bread crumbs and rosemary. Do not overblend as it will become pasty. Set aside.

Lay the breasts between two sheets of wax paper and pound them lightly. Lay the flattened breasts skin side down on a work surface. Spread 1 teaspoon of Pesto on each breast and sprinkle with a little pepper. Place one fourth of the stuffing in the center of each and top with a slice of prosciutto. Roll the chicken around the stuffing and secure with a toothpick.

Heat the butter in a skillet and brown the breasts on all sides. Add the wine and stock, cover, and simmer for 7 minutes. Remove the breasts from the pan and keep them warm. Simmer the sauce for 5 minutes more, then set aside.

In another skillet, heat the cream. Add the remaining 2 tablespoons of Pesto, the sherry and the sauce to the cream, whisking constantly. Simmer for 3 minutes or until the sauce is slightly thickened.

Remove the toothpicks from the chicken and cut the breasts into ½-inch-thick slices. To do this, place the stuffed breast, seam side down, on a cutting board. Using a sharp knife, slice from top to bottom slightly on the diagonal. The stuffing will remain intact and you will have a circle of white chicken meat around the colorful stuffing. You should have about 5 round slices. Arrange these on the plate by overlapping the slices slightly. Pour the cream sauce over the chicken slices and serve immediately.

◆————————◆

A young lawyer named Al Rottman and his wife Naomi used to spend their vacations in Hyannis. A friend of theirs, a reviewer for Diners Club, told them that one of the best restaurants on the Cape was CIRO & SAL'S in Provincetown. That was 1958, and they have been coming back ever since. Mr. Rottman is now a superior court judge for the State of Connecticut. The Rottmans pick the Pollo al Bergamo as their favorite dish.

POLLO AL BERGAMO

Chicken Breast Stuffed with Sausage

SERVES 4

4	large chicken breasts, boned but not skinned
6	Italian sweet sausages, cooked, skinned and coarsely chopped
¾	cup thinly sliced fresh mushrooms
¼	cup slivered blanched almonds
1½	tablespoons dried basil
2	teaspoons dried fennel seeds, crushed
1	tablespoon garlic, finely chopped
	Salt and freshly ground black pepper
⅓	cup clarified butter (page 223)
2	tablespoons olive oil
2	garlic cloves
½	cup dry white wine
1	cup Balsamella (page 192)
1	tablespoon finely chopped fresh parsley or basil leaves

Lay the breasts between two sheets of wax paper and pound them lightly. Lay the flattened breasts skin side down on a work surface. In the center of each fillet place one fourth each of the sausage meat, mushrooms and almonds, and a sprinkle of the basil, fennel, garlic, salt and pepper. Fold the chicken over the stuffing and pin together with a toothpick.

Heat the butter and oil in a large skillet. Add the garlic cloves and sauté until golden, then remove and discard. Add the stuffed chicken breasts and brown them on all sides. Add the wine and cook for another 10 minutes, turning the breasts continually (be careful not to tear the skin).

Transfer the cooked breasts to a cutting board. Remove the toothpicks and slice each breast as for the Petto di Pollo con Broccoli recipe. Lay the slices on a warm serving dish and pour the Balsamella, which should be hot, along the center of the rounds. Garnish with parsley or fresh basil leaves and serve immediately.

POLLO IN PADELLA

Chicken Breast Stuffed with Mushrooms and Herbs

SERVES 4

4	large chicken breasts, boned but not skinned
4	thin slices mozzarella
½	cup thinly sliced fresh mushrooms
1½	cups bread crumbs
⅔	cup freshly grated Parmigiano
2	tablespoons finely chopped fresh parsley leaves
1	tablespoon dried basil
1½	teaspoons finely chopped garlic
¼	teaspoon chopped fresh thyme leaves or dried thyme
½	cup clarified butter (page 223)
¼	cup olive oil
¾	cup dry white wine
1	tablespoon lemon juice
1	large egg
	Dash of Tabasco sauce
	Salt and freshly ground black pepper
4	thin slices prosciutto
½	cup chicken stock (page 51)

Lay the breasts between 2 sheets of wax paper and pound them lightly. Lay the flattened breasts skin side down on a work surface. Place 1 slice of mozzarella and 4 or 5 mushroom slices on each breast.

Make the stuffing. In a mixing bowl, combine the bread crumbs, grated cheese, parsley, basil, ½ teaspoon of the garlic, thyme, ¼ cup of the butter, 2 tablespoons of the olive oil, ¼ cup of the wine, lemon juice, egg, Tabasco sauce and salt and pepper to taste.

Place 3 or 4 tablespoons of the stuffing in the center of each breast and cover the stuffing with a slice of prosciutto. Roll the chicken over the stuffing and secure with a toothpick.

Heat the remaining butter and oil in a skillet and brown the rolled breasts on all sides. Lower the heat and add the remaining wine and garlic. Season with salt and pepper and simmer for 7 minutes.

Remove the breasts from the pan and put them on a warm plate and keep warm. Add the chicken stock to the juices in the pan and simmer for 3 minutes. Season with salt and pepper, if necessary.

Remove the toothpicks from the breasts and slice the chicken as for the Petto di Pollo con Broccoli recipe. Arrange the slices on a warm serving dish and pour the sauce over them. Serve immediately.

POLLO AL CASIMELLO

Sautéed Chicken with Prosciutto and Madeira

SERVES 4

4	whole chicken breasts, boned and skinned
½	cup clarified butter (page 223)
10	thin slices prosciutto, diced
4	garlic cloves, pressed
½	cup dry Madeira
½	cup Espagnole Sauce (page 195)
½	teaspoon dried savory
	Freshly ground black pepper
10	thin slices mozzarella, chopped
4	tablespoons finely chopped fresh parsley leaves

Cut the breasts in half. Then cut each piece in half on the bias. Lay the pieces between two sheets of wax paper and pound until very thin.

Heat the butter in a large skillet and sauté the prosciutto lightly. Add the chicken and garlic and brown the chicken on both sides. Transfer the chicken to a warm plate.

Add the Madeira, Espagnole sauce, savory and pepper to the pan. Simmer for 3 minutes. Return the chicken to the pan and simmer for a minute on each side. Sprinkle the mozzarella over the chicken. Cover the pan and cook just until the cheese has melted. Sprinkle with the parsley and serve at once.

POLLO ALLA GENOVESE

Chicken with Herbs and Vegetables

SERVES 4

4   *chicken breasts, boned but not skinned*
    Dried rosemary or chopped fresh rosemary leaves
    Dried basil or chopped fresh basil leaves
    Ground nutmeg
    Finely chopped garlic
    Finely chopped fresh sage
    Dried tarragon or chopped fresh tarragon leaves
    Dried thyme or chopped fresh thyme leaves
4   *tablespoons freshly grated Parmigiano*
4   *teaspoons finely chopped fresh parsley leaves*
12 *fresh mushrooms, stem ends trimmed*
4   *teaspoons butter*
1   *carrot, finely chopped*
1   *celery stalk, finely chopped*
1   *large onion, finely chopped*
⅔   *cup clarified butter (page 223)*
½   *cup dry white wine*
¼   *cup chicken stock (page 51)*
8   *¼-inch-thick slices eggplant, cut from the length of the eggplant*
8   *artichoke hearts, lightly steamed*
¼   *lemon*
    Salt and freshly ground black pepper

Lay the breasts between two sheets of wax paper and pound them lightly. Lay the flattened breasts skin side down on a work surface. Sprinkle each with a pinch of all the herbs. In the center, put 1 tablespoon of the Parmigiano, 1 teaspoon of the parsley, 2 or 3 whole mushrooms and 1 teaspoon of butter. Roll the chicken over the filling and secure with 2 toothpicks.

Heat 6 tablespoons of the clarified butter in a skillet. Add the breasts and brown them on all sides. Lower the heat and add the carrot, celery, onion, wine and stock. Cook for 10 minutes. Add the artichoke hearts and cook for 5 minutes more. Strain the sauce from the pan and set it aside. Keep the sauce and chicken warm.

Lay the eggplant strips on a buttered baking sheet, brush their tops with clarified butter and broil until light brown. Arrange the eggplant on a warm serving dish.

Remove the toothpicks from the chicken and slice each breast as for the Petto di Pollo con Broccoli recipe. Lay the slices over the eggplant. Arrange the artichoke hearts and the chopped vegetables around the chicken. Pour the sauce over both the chicken and the vegetables and serve immediately.

POLLO ALLA ZINGARELLA

Chicken with Piquant Sauce

SERVES 4

4	8-ounce chicken breasts, boned and skinned
	Salt and freshly ground black pepper
2	tablespoons olive oil
2	tablespoons butter
½	cup chopped scallions (white and tender green parts)
2	tablespoons all-purpose flour
1	small garlic clove, crushed
½	cup dry white wine
2	tablespoons tomato paste (diluted with 4 tablespoons of the wine)
½	cup white wine vinegar
2	tablespoons capers, rinsed, drained and finely chopped
8	anchovy fillets, rinsed, dried and finely chopped
4	small pickled onions, chopped
½	garlic clove, finely chopped
3	tablespoons finely chopped fresh parsley leaves

Lay the breasts between 2 sheets of wax paper and pound them lightly. Season them with salt and pepper.

Heat the oil and butter in a skillet. Add the scallions and sauté until they soften. Add the breasts and brown them on both sides, then sprinkle them with the flour. Add the garlic and wine and let the wine reduce by half, then add the diluted tomato paste, salt and pepper.

Lower the heat and cook for 5 minutes. Remove the breasts from the pan and keep them warm. Continue to cook the pan juices over low heat for 10 minutes.

While that is cooking, make the second part of your sauce in another pan. Simmer the wine vinegar until it is reduced slightly. Add the remaining ingredients and simmer for another 2 minutes.

Return the chicken to the original skillet. Pour the sauce from the second pan over the chicken. Stir gently, to mix the two sauces.

Arrange the chicken on a warm serving plate, and pour the sauce over the breasts. Serve immediately.

POLLO ALLA FIORENTINA
Sautéed Chicken Breast with Mushrooms and Spinach

SERVES 6

6	whole chicken breasts, boned but not skinned
6	small shallots, finely chopped
6	scallions (white and tender green parts), thinly sliced
	Freshly ground nutmeg
2	cups dry white wine
5	cups chicken stock
1	pound fresh spinach, tough stems removed
8	tablespoons butter
1	cup thinly sliced domestic mushrooms
1	cup heavy cream
	Salt and freshly ground white pepper

Lay the chicken breasts between two sheets of wax paper and pound them lightly. Season the skinless side with salt, pepper and nutmeg. Sprinkle each breast with the shallots and scallions. Fold each breast into an envelope shape (they should be as large as possible).

Combine the wine and stock in a pan and heat slowly. Poach the breasts, seam side down, in the wine and stock until done (about 10 to 15 minutes). Remove the breasts from the pan and keep them warm. Strain the poaching liquid into a new pan. Bring the liquid to a boil and let it reduce by half.

While this is reducing, prepare the vegetables. Heat the butter in a skillet and sauté the mushrooms until tender. Season with salt and pepper, remove the mushrooms from the pan and add the spinach (if necessary, add more butter to the pan before adding the spinach). Sauté the spinach just until tender and season with salt, pepper and nutmeg. Arrange the spinach over the bottom of a warm serving plate. Sprinkle the mushrooms over the spinach.

Now add the cream to the reduced stock-wine sauce. Season with salt and pepper and simmer for 3 minutes.

Arrange the chicken breasts, either whole or sliced, on the bed of vegetables. Pour the sauce over all.

FEGATINI DI POLLO
Chicken Livers Sautéed with White Wine and Basil

SERVES 4

½   cup clarified butter (page 223)
2   pounds chicken livers, cleaned and cut into halves
½   lemon
6   tablespoons dry white wine
1   teaspoon dried basil or chopped fresh basil leaves
    Salt and freshly ground black pepper
4   tablespoons finely chopped fresh parsley leaves

Heat the butter in a large skillet and brown the livers over a high flame. Squeeze the lemon juice into the pan, add the remaining ingredients and cook for 2 to 3 minutes. If you desire them well done, reduce the heat and continue cooking.

The fegatini may also be made with mushrooms. Simply add a handful of sliced mushrooms to the livers at the beginning of the cooking.

Either fegatini preparation is excellent served with spaghetti. Cook the spaghetti in salted boiling water until *al dente*. Drain it and transfer it to a warm serving bowl. Pour the fegatini and its sauce over the spaghetti and toss lightly.

FEGATINI DI POLLO CON SALVIA
Sautéed Chicken Livers with Sage and Prosciutto

SERVES 4

2	tablespoons butter
1	cup bread crumbs
1	teaspoon finely chopped garlic
1	teaspoon dried basil
1	teaspoon finely chopped fresh parsley leaves
	Salt and freshly ground black pepper
6	tablespoons clarified butter (page 223)
6	thin slices prosciutto, chopped
2	pounds chicken livers, cleaned and cut into halves
2	garlic cloves, finely chopped
1	teaspoon dried thyme
4	leaves fresh sage, chopped
6	tablespoons Marsala
½	lemon
4	thin slices prosciutto
2	tablespoons freshly grated Parmigiano

Preheat the broiler.

Melt the butter in a skillet, then add the bread crumbs, 1 teaspoon garlic, basil, parsley and salt and pepper to taste. Toast the crumbs until golden and set them aside.

Heat the clarified butter in another skillet and brown the chopped prosciutto lightly. Add the livers, garlic, thyme, sage, pepper and Marsala. Cook for 1 minute. Squeeze the lemon juice into the pan.

Transfer the livers and sauce to an ovenproof dish. Lay the slices of prosciutto over the livers and sprinkle with the seasoned bread crumbs and Parmigiano. Broil until the crumbs are browned. Serve immediately.

CARNE

Meat

Franz Kline was seated at the family table one day and commented that when he was young and struggling, he lived hard and drank rot gut. Now that he was successful, he was too old to live the fast life, and he could no longer drink. "But," he said, "I can still drive." So out he went and bought himself a Ferrari.

MAIALE NEL FUOCO ALLA GENOVINA
Genovina's Pork Cooked Over the Fire

This method of cooking not only pork, but also beef, veal, chicken and salt cod (pre-soaked) was taught to me by a dear friend in Capodimonte, a small lakeside town north of Rome. As the cool weather arrived she would light a fire in the fireplace, and on a small grating which she placed over the hot embers, she would cook all of the above foods as well as slices of her homemade pecorino cheese.

Heat your grill or broiler. The meat or chicken should be cut into individual portions (chops work very well). Rub salt and pepper into the meat. If desired, crushed fennel seed may also be rubbed into the meat.

Pour some olive oil onto a plate. Cut a clove of garlic in half and add it to the oil. Take a long, full sprig of fresh rosemary and coat it in the oil.

Place the meat on the grill. As it is cooking, baste it with the rosemary dipped in the oil. (Dip the sprig in the oil and pass it lightly over the meat.) Turn the meat once and cook to desired doneness.

COSCIOTTO DI VITELLO
Roast Leg of Veal with Fennel and Cream

SERVINGS WILL DEPEND ON SIZE OF VEAL LEG

1	veal leg, bone in
	Butter
	Freshly ground black pepper
	About a handful of fresh sage leaves
½	pound pancetta
2	large carrots, peeled and cut into large chunks
1	large onion, cut into large pieces
1	head fresh fennel (bulb only), cut into large pieces
1	tablespoon dried basil
	Salt
3	cups (approximately) veal stock
1	cup (approximately) dry white wine

1   cup heavy cream
1   cup buttermilk, sour cream or crème fraîche

Preheat the oven to 425 degrees.

Trim the fat from the leg and dress it. Rub butter and black pepper over the entire leg. Slice a pocket in the leg and stuff it with the sage.

In a large heavy skillet, cook the pancetta over moderate heat until it gives up its fat (this is called "rendering"). Remove the pieces of meat, add the veal to the skillet and brown it on all sides in the fat.

Place the leg on a rack in a roasting pan. Surround it with the vegetables. Sprinkle the basil, salt and pepper over the vegetables and roast for 15 minutes. Lower the oven temperature to 325 degrees and continue to roast, allowing 15 minutes per pound. Baste with the veal stock and wine throughout the roasting period.

Remove the veal from the pan and cover it to keep it warm while you prepare the sauce.

Place the roasting pan on your stove burners and bring the juices in the pan to a boil. Scrape the sides and bottom of the pan and mix these particles in with the juices. Let boil for 2 minutes. Strain the juices through cheesecloth into a heavy saucepan and bring them to a boil. Whisk in the cream and stir over moderate heat for 2 minutes. Whisk in the buttermilk, sour cream or crème fraîche. Allow the sauce to reduce by ½.

Slice the leg. To do so, hold the leg by the shank and slice down and around. Make the slices 6- or 7-inches long and ¼-inch thick. Slices should not exceed 3 inches across. Overlap the slices on a hot plate and pour some of the sauce over the meat. Serve immediately.

ARROSTO DI VITELLO

Roasted Loin of Veal Stuffed with Prosciutto and Watercress

SERVES 10 TO 12

2   cups fresh bread crumbs
     Milk
2   pounds Italian sweet sausage, removed from the casing and
         puréed in a blender
1   pound veal, ground and then puréed in a blender
1   chicken breast, ground and puréed in a blender
3   fresh eggs, lightly beaten
10   sage leaves, chopped
2   tablespoons finely chopped fresh parsley leaves
     Salt and freshly ground black pepper
1   8- to 9-pound veal loin (weight with bone in).
12   thin slices prosciutto
1   bunch watercress, all thick stems removed
1   cup olive oil or rendered pork fat
     Caul fat or thinly sliced pork fat, enough to wrap around the
         loin
2   onions, coarsely chopped
2   celery stalks, coarsely chopped
1   bunch carrots, finely chopped
8   cups dry white wine
8   cups veal stock
6   sage leaves

Preheat the oven to 300 degrees.

To make the forcemeat, combine the bread crumbs and enough milk to cover in a large bowl. Allow the bread to absorb all the milk. Add the sausage, veal, chicken, eggs, sage and parsley to the softened bread crumbs. Season with a generous amount of salt and pepper. Mix thoroughly and set aside.

Butterfly the veal loin or have the butcher do it for you, and lay it out flat. Season the inside of the loin with salt and pepper. Lay six slices of prosciutto over half the loin. Form the forcemeat into a loaf shape and place it on the prosciutto (see Note). Now lay the watercress down the center of the loaf and cover with the remaining 6 slices of prosciutto. Fold the other half of the loin over the forcemeat and roll the loin so that it fits snugly around the forcemeat. Sew the seams together. Tie the loin securely and then rub the outside with salt and pepper.

Heat the oil or fat in a large pan and brown the veal on all sides. If using sliced pork fat, blanch it before wrapping it around the loin. Otherwise, wrap the caul fat securely around the loin and tie it once again.

Spread the onions, celery and carrots over the bottom of a roasting pan and lay the loin on top. Add the wine and stock to the pan and roast for 45 minutes, basting occasionally.

Remove the veal from the pan and place it in a warm spot. Strain the vegetables from the pan and purée them. Combine the purée with the remaining pan juices in a saucepan and heat slowly. If the sauce is too thick, add more veal stock. Season with the sage leaves and more salt and pepper. Simmer for 5 minutes. Serve the sauce with the sliced veal.

NOTE: Extra forcemeat may be shaped into small loaves and cooked with the roast. This forcemeat is delightful served with fettuccine that has been tossed in the sauce from the roast.

VITELLO ALLA SFORZA
Broiled Veal Chop with Espagnole Sauce

SERVES 4

4   *10-ounce veal chops, pounded lightly*
     Salt and freshly ground black pepper
½   *cup clarified butter (page 223)*
     Juice of one lemon
1⅓ *cup Espagnole Sauce (page 195)*

Preheat the broiler.

Rub salt and pepper into each veal chop. Combine the butter and lemon juice in an ovenproof baking pan. Add the chops to the pan and turn to coat the chops with the butter.

Broil the chops on each side until they are firm to the touch. Just before they are done, drain the fat from the pan and add the Espagnole Sauce. Cook just until the chops are done and the sauce is warm.

OSSOBUCO
Braised Veal Shank in Espagnole Sauce

SERVES 4

½   *cup all-purpose flour*
     Salt and freshly ground black pepper
4   *veal shanks, 2 inches in diameter and tied with a string across*
     the middle (This keeps the meat around the bone.)
¼   *cup olive oil*
¼   *cup clarified butter (page 223)*
2   *carrots, cut into small dice*
1   *celery stalk, cut into small dice*
1   *onion, finely chopped*
1   *garlic clove, finely chopped*
½   *cup dry white wine*
1   *bay leaf*
½   *cup Espagnole Sauce (page 195)*

½   cup veal stock (page 50)
2   cups Italian peeled plum tomatoes, drained, seeded and chopped
2   tablespoons finely chopped fresh parsley leaves
1   recipe of Risotto alla Milanese (page 92)

Preheat the oven to 325 degrees.

Season the flour with a little salt and pepper. Dredge the shanks in the flour, then shake to remove any excess.

Heat the oil in a skillet and brown the shanks well on all sides. Drain on paper towels.

Heat the butter in another skillet and add the carrots, celery, onion and garlic. Sauté for 5 minutes. Add the wine and bay leaf and cook for 5 minutes more.

In a baking pan just large enough to hold the shanks, spread the vegetable mixture over the bottom of the pan. Lay the veal shanks over the vegetables and add the Espagnole Sauce, stock, tomatoes and parsley. Bake, uncovered, for 2½ hours, turning and basting the veal every 30 minutes.

Remove the string from the shanks, being careful to keep the meat around the bone. Spread the Risotto Milanese over a warm serving platter. Arrange the shanks in the center of the rice and pour the sauce from the baking pan over all.

VITELLO ALLA FILOMENA

Marinated Veal Baked with Eggplant and Tomatoes

SERVES 6

2 cups red wine vinegar
2 cups water
1 cup extra virgin olive oil
2 garlic cloves, crushed
1 onion, finely chopped
1 tablespoon dried basil
1 bay leaf
½ teaspoon freshly ground black pepper
3 pounds boneless veal, trimmed and cut into 1-inch cubes
¾ cup olive oil
1 tablespoon finely chopped garlic
½ cup clarified butter (page 223)
2 eggplants (about 1½ pounds each)
1½ cups Espagnole Sauce (page 195)
1½ cups freshly grated Parmigiano
3 cups Italian plum tomatoes, drained, seeded and diced
    Salt and freshly ground black pepper

Start marinade 3 to 4 days in advance.

Combine the first 8 ingredients in a bowl. Add the veal cubes, cover and marinate in the refrigerator for 3 or 4 days. Stir every 12 hours. Drain well before using.

Preheat the oven to 375 degrees.

Heat ½ cup of the olive oil in a skillet. Add the garlic and veal and brown the veal cubes on all sides. Remove them from the pan and drain them on paper towels. Set them aside.

Cut the ends off the eggplants and then cut each eggplant in half lengthwise. Lay them cut side down and cut them along their lengths into ¼-inch slices. Discard the end slices. Brush each slice with a little of the clarified butter and lay them on a baking sheet. Bake the eggplant slices until they are light brown. Drain the eggplant on paper towels. Do not turn off the oven.

Combine the veal and Espagnole Sauce in a bowl and toss to coat the cubes. Drain the sauce from the bowl and reserve.

Grease the bottom of a 9- by 13- by 2-inch roasting pan with the remaining oil and butter. Cover the bottom of the pan with eggplant slices. Sprinkle the eggplant with a little salt, pepper and Parmigiano. Spread one third of the tomatoes over the eggplant and sprinkle some of the basil on the tomatoes. Cover the tomatoes with a layer of veal cubes. Cover the veal with a layer of eggplant and repeat the process. The last layer should be tomatoes. (Be sure to reserve ½ cup of the Parmigiano for the topping.) Pour the reserved Espagnole Sauce over the tomatoes and top with the remaining Parmigiano. (This process may also be done in individual ceramic baking dishes.)

Cover the veal with aluminum foil and bake for 35 minutes.

SCALOPPINI CON SENAPE
Sautéed Veal in Mustard Sauce

SERVES 4

1¼ pounds boneless veal top round or rump
¼   cup clarified butter (page 223)
1   cup thinly sliced mushrooms
½   teaspoon dried basil
¼   teaspoon dried thyme
2   tablespoons brandy
¼   cup dry red wine
1   tablespoon Dijon mustard
1   tablespoon capers, rinsed and drained
    Salt and freshly ground black pepper

Cutting across the grain, slice the veal into ¼-inch-thick wafers. Pound the veal gently between sheets of wax paper.

Heat the butter in a skillet and sauté the veal until lightly browned on both sides. Add the mushrooms, basil, thyme and half of the brandy. Let the brandy burn off, then add the red wine and cook for 1 minute. Remove the veal to a warm serving plate.

Stir the mustard into the sauce. Add the remaining brandy, capers, salt and pepper. Reduce until slightly thickened. Spoon the mushrooms and sauce over the veal and serve immediately.

VITELLO ALLA MILANESE
Breaded Veal Sautéed with Garlic and Lemon

SERVES 4

2　large eggs, beaten
2　tablespoons milk
　　Salt and freshly ground black pepper
1　cup bread crumbs
4　7-ounce veal cutlets, cut ¼ inch thick
½　cup olive oil
1　teaspoon finely chopped garlic
4　lemon wedges

Beat the eggs and milk together in a shallow pan. Season with salt and pepper and set it aside.

Place the bread crumbs in another shallow pan and season with salf and pepper. Set them aside.

Lay the veal cutlets between sheets of wax paper and pound until very thin. Dip each cutlet in the egg wash (let any excess egg drip off) and then coat the cutlets with the bread crumbs, pressing lightly with your hand to make sure the crumbs adhere to the meat. Shake off any excess crumbs. Refrigerate for 2 hours before cooking.

Heat the oil in a large skillet over moderate heat. Add the cutlets and the garlic and sauté until golden on each side.

Transfer the cutlets to paper towels to drain. Serve immediately on a warm platter with the lemon wedges.

VITELLO ALLA PARMIGIANA
Veal with Parmigiano and Ragù

SERVES 4

4　7-ounce veal cutlets, breaded and fried as for Vitello alla
　　Milanese
1½　cups Ragù (page 88), heated
4　tablespoons freshly grated Parmigiano
12　thin (1-by 3-inch) slices of mozzarella

Preheat the broiler.

Arrange the cutlets on an ovenproof platter. Cover each with the Ragù, but do not flood the cutlets in the sauce. Sprinkle each cutlet with 1 tablespoon of the Parmigiano, then place 3 slices of the mozzarella on each.

Broil just until the cheese melts.

SALTIMBOCCA ALLA ROMANA
Veal Rolls Stuffed with Prosciutto and Mozzarella

SERVES 6

12 thin slices veal, pounded
12 thin slices prosciutto
12 thin slices mozzarella
3   tablespoons dried basil or chopped fresh basil leaves
2   teaspoons chopped fresh sage leaves
    Freshly ground black pepper
4   tablespoons cream sherry
6   tablespoons clarified butter (page 223)
½   cup dry white wine
6   teaspoons fresh lemon juice
2   teaspoons finely chopped fresh parsley leaves
    Salt and freshly ground black pepper
6   lemon wedges for garnish

Lay the slices of veal on a work surface. Place a slice of prosciutto and a slice of mozzarella on each. Sprinkle with a little of the basil, sage and black pepper. Roll up the veal tightly into cylinders and fasten with a toothpick.

Heat a skillet over high heat and pour the sherry into the hot pan, tipping the pan to coat the bottom evenly. Add the butter and, when it is hot, brown the veal rolls completely. Add the white wine, lemon juice and parsley to the pan and season with salt and pepper. Lower the heat and cook for 10 to 15 minutes.

Transfer the veal rolls to a warm serving dish and garnish with lemon wedges.

VITELLO PICCATO

Sautéed Veal with Mushrooms and Cream

SERVES 4

½   cup clarified butter (page 223)
20 ounces veal wafers (see recipe for Scaloppine alla Marsala)
1   cup thinly sliced fresh mushrooms
1   teaspoon finely chopped garlic
2   teaspoons fresh lemon juice
    Salt and freshly ground black pepper
½   cup dry white wine
1   cup veal stock (page 50)
    Juice of 1 lemon
1   cup heavy cream

Heat the butter in a large skillet. Add the veal, mushrooms and ½ teaspoon of the garlic, and brown the veal lightly on both sides. Add the lemon juice and salt and pepper. Transfer the veal and mushrooms to a warm serving platter and keep them warm while you make the sauce.

Add the wine to the pan and bring it to a boil over high heat. Continue boiling it for 1 minute. Add the veal stock, lemon juice, remaining garlic and salt and pepper to taste. Boil for 3 to 4 minutes. Add the heavy cream and simmer for another 4 minutes, or until the sauce is slightly thickened. Add more salt and pepper if necessary. Pour this sauce over the veal and mushrooms and serve immediately.

MEDAGLIONI DI VITELLO

Sautéed Medallions of Veal in Brandy-Butter Sauce

SERVES 4

1   *cup all-purpose flour*
     Salt and freshly ground black pepper
24 *ounces veal, cut into ⅜-inch-thick medallions*
6   *tablespoons clarified butter (page 223)*
4   *tablespoons brandy*
6   *tablespoons Espagnole Sauce (page 195)*
2   *tablespoons butter, softened*

Season the flour with a pinch of salt and pepper. Dredge the medallions in the flour and shake off any excess.

Heat the clarified butter in a skillet. Add the medallions and brown on both sides. Add the brandy and Espagnole Sauce and cook for about 5 minutes over medium heat.

Transfer the veal to a warm serving platter and keep it warm. Over high heat, add salt and pepper to taste, and whisk the butter quickly into the sauce. Pour the sauce over the medallions and serve immediately.

One day, while Ciro and I were driving to New Bedford to have the new menus of the season printed, he mentioned he would like to replace one of the veal dishes. We threw ideas at each other, and when I suggested veal with chicken livers, he agreed. As we rode on, he added prosciutto, Port Salut and a wine sauce. By the time we arrived at the printer, he had given it a name, Noce di Vitello alla Bolognese, and a description.

A few weeks later the menus arrived and people started ordering the new veal dish. Ciro shrugged and said, "I guess I'll have to make it now." Port Salut is very pungent when it is cooked, and when waiter Joe DeRocco first smelled it, he said, "It's obscene! I won't serve it!" Nonetheless, it was a hit from the very beginning. The Port Salut was eventually replaced with a combination of mozzarella and esrom.

—AL DiLAURO

NOCE DI VITELLO ALLA BOLOGNESE

Veal and Chicken Livers Sautéed with Prosciutto and Esrom

SERVES 4

1⅓ cups cream sherry
⅔ cup water
2 garlic cloves, finely chopped
   Freshly ground black pepper
1 pound veal, thinly sliced
⅔ cup clarified butter (page 223)
6 chicken livers, cleaned and coarsely chopped
1 teaspoon dried basil
   Pinch of dried thyme
2 garlic cloves, finely chopped
   Salt and freshly ground black pepper
6 thin slices prosciutto, trimmed of excess fat
6 thin (1½-by 3-inch) slices of mozzarella
6 thin (1½-by 3-inch) slices of esrom
4 tablespoons dry white wine
2 tablespoons finely chopped fresh parsley leaves

Start the marinade the day before.

Combine the first 4 ingredients in a bowl and add the veal. Be sure that the veal is completely covered with the marinade. Cover the bowl and refrigerate overnight.

When ready to serve, heat the butter in a skillet and brown the livers lightly. Add the veal, basil, thyme, garlic, salt and pepper to the pan. Brown the veal quickly on both sides. Cover the veal and livers with the prosciutto, then lay the mozzarella and esrom cheeses alternately over the prosciutto. Add the wine, cover the pan and cook until the cheeses melt. Sprinkle with the parsley and serve immediately.

MEDAGLIONI DI VITELLO CON PORCINI E PEPERONI

Medallions of Veal with Porcini and Peppers

SERVES 4

½   cup dried porcini mushrooms or any fresh wild mushrooms
1   large sweet red pepper
24   ounces veal medallions (from rib eye) cut ¾-inch-thick
4   tablespoons clarified butter (page 223)
½   cup Barolo wine
2   tablespoons demi-glacé
8   whole savory leaves
     Salt and greshly ground black pepper

Cover the porcini mushrooms with tepid water and let them soak for 1 hour. Drain and rinse the mushrooms, then cut them into thin slices. If using fresh mushrooms, simply clean and cut them into thin slices.

Scorch the skin of the pepper over a flame of the burner (or broiler). Peel the skin and cut the pepper into ¼-inch-wide strips.

Pound the medallions lightly.

Heat the butter in a skillet. Add the medallions and brown them on both sides. Add the wine and demi-glacé and reduce for 1 minute. Add the red pepper and simmer for 2 minutes. Add the mushrooms, savory and salt and pepper to taste.

Remove the medallions to a warm serving plate. Continue to reduce the sauce until it is a syrupy consistency; then spoon it over the veal and serve immediately.

SCALOPPINE DI VITELLO ALLA MARSALA
Veal Sautéed with Marsala

SERVES 4

1⅓   cups cream sherry
⅔   cup water
2   garlic cloves, finely chopped
      Freshly ground black pepper
20   ounces veal wafers (see Note)
½   cup clarified butter (page 223)
⅔   cup dry sherry
1⅓   cups thinly sliced fresh mushrooms
½   lemon
4   tablespoons Marsala
1   teaspoon finely chopped garlic
2   teaspoons dried basil
2   tablespoons finely chopped fresh parsley leaves
4   lemon wedges for garnish

Start the marinade the day before.

Combine the first 4 ingredients in a bowl and add the veal wafers. Be sure the veal is covered completely with the marinade. Cover the bowl and refrigerate overnight.

Heat a large skillet over high heat. Add 4 tablespoons of the dry sherry to the hot pan, tipping the pan so that the sherry coats the bottom evenly. Add the clarified butter and heat it. Add the veal and the mushrooms to the pan and sauté the veal very quickly on both sides. Remove the veal and mushrooms from the pan and keep them warm.

Keeping the pan on high heat, squeeze the lemon juice into the pan, then add the remaining sherry, Marsala, garlic and basil and cook over high heat until it is reduced to a syrupy consistency. Return the veal to the pan and coat it quickly with the sauce.

Arrange the veal on a warm serving dish and add the sauce and chopped parsley. Serve immediately with the lemon wedges.

NOTE: The perfect cut of the veal for this preparation comes from the top round of the leg. Once this piece has been freed from its membrane and connective tissue, it is cut across the grain into ⅛-inch-thick slices.

BISTECCA CON PORCINI
Beefsteak with Porcini and Brandy

SERVES 4

2   ounces dried porcini mushrooms
4   cups tepid water
4   16-ounce New York shell steaks, trimmed of excess fat (Leave
         ¼-inch of fat.)
         Salt and freshly ground black pepper
4   tablespoons clarified butter (page 223)
4   garlic cloves, finely chopped
4   teaspoons finely chopped shallots
½   cup brandy
½   cup beef stock (page 49)
2 to 4   tablespoons butter, softened

Cover the porcini with the tepid water and let them soak for 1 hour. Remove the porcini and rinse them very well. Cut them into thin slices. Strain the soaking liquid through several layers of paper towels and reserve it.

Preheat the broiler.

Rub salt and pepper into both sides of each steak. Broil them, turning once, to the desired doneness.

While the steaks are cooking, prepare the sauce. Heat the clarified butter in a saucepan. Add the garlic and shallots and sauté for 30 seconds. Add the brandy and allow it to burn off, about 1 minute. Add the porcini, stock and ¼ cup of the soaking liquid from the mushrooms. Allow to reduce over high heat for 2 minutes or until thickened.

Transfer the steaks to a warm serving dish.

Add the butter to the sauce and lower the heat to moderate. Quickly whisk the butter into the sauce, pour it over the steak and serve immediately.

NOTE: This sauce is also excellent with grilled veal chops. Simply substitute veal stock for the beef stock.

BISTECCA ALLA PIEMONTESE
Beefsteak Broiled with Mushrooms and Red Wine

SERVES 4

4	16-ounce New York shell steaks, trimmed (Leave ½ inch of fat.)
6	tablespoons clarified butter (page 223)
4	garlic cloves, pressed
	Salt and freshly ground black pepper
1	cup thinly sliced fresh mushrooms
½	cup dry red wine
2	teaspoons fresh lemon juice

Preheat the broiler.

Rub both sides of the steaks with the butter, garlic, salt and pepper. Place the steaks in a shallow pan. Broil until one side of the steak is well browned. Turn them over, add the remaining ingredients and broil to the desired doneness.

Transfer the steaks to a warm serving dish and top with the mushrooms and pan juices.

FILETTI DI BUE CAPRICCIOSI
Fillets of Beef with a Little of Everything

SERVES 4

MARINADE

2	tablespoons extra virgin olive oil
½	cup dry red wine
2	teaspoons dry mustard
8	whole black peppercorns
1	teaspoon dried basil
1	teaspoon chopped fresh ginger
4	4-ounce beef fillets

SAUCE

4   anchovy fillets, rinsed and dried
4   tablespoons chopped green olives
8   fresh basil leaves
2   teaspoons dry mustard
1½   cups dry red wine
4   slices pancetta
      Salt and freshly ground black pepper

Mix together all the ingredients for the marinade in a bowl. Add the beef and marinate at room temperature for 2 to 4 hours.

Blend the anchovy fillets, olives, basil, mustard and ¼ cup of the wine until smooth.

Remove the beef from the marinade and rub it with salt and pepper.

In a heavy skillet, render the fat from the pancetta. Remove the pieces of meat. Add the beef and brown for 2 minutes on each side. Spread the anchovy-olive paste on the top of the fillets. Continue to cook over moderate heat to the desired doneness.

Remove the beef from the pan. Scrape any pieces of meat from the pan. Add the remaining red wine and let it reduce until syrupy. Season with salt and pepper and pour the sauce onto a warm plate. Arrange the beef fillets on top and serve immediately.

◆———————◆

Sometimes in the afternoon we would go to the restaurant to help Ciro and Sal do prep work like grating cheese and bread crumbs by hand, chopping onions and rolling meatballs. One day I was rolling meatballs. Sal said they were too small. Then Ciro came by and said they were too big (he hated big meatballs). Then Sal came by again—too small. Then Ciro—too big. Another day, I don't remember who was responsible, the meatball mixture was not properly mixed. Some poor customer got a meatball with about twenty raisins. The next day, using quantity control, we rolled each meatball and then pressed two raisins into each, like a double navel.

—AL DiLAURO

POLPETTE

Meatballs

MAKES 12 MEATBALLS

2	tablespoons olive oil
1½	cups bread crumbs
1	cup milk
1	pound lean ground beef
2	large eggs
½	cup dark raisins
½	teaspoon finely chopped garlic
2	tablespoons dried basil
¼	cup finely chopped fresh parsley leaves
⅓	cup freshly grated Parmigiano
	Salt and freshly ground black pepper

Preheat the oven to 400 degrees.

Coat the bottom of a baking pan with the olive oil.

Mix the bread crumbs with the milk in a bowl and let them stand to absorb the milk.

Add the remaining ingredients to the bowl and mix well.

Use a tablespoon to scoop out the mixture. Form into 1-inch balls. Arrange the meatballs in the pan and add ¼ cup of water to prevent the meat from sticking to the pan.

Bake for about 20 minutes. If desired, transfer the meatballs to another pan, add some Ragù (page 88) and bake for 10 minutes more.

AGNELLO AI FERRI CON CARCIOFI FRITTI
Broiled Lamb Chops with Fried Artichokes

SERVES 4

1	cup dry sherry
	Juice of 1 lemon
4	tablespoons extra virgin olive oil
2	garlic cloves, finely chopped
1	teaspoon chopped fresh rosemary leaves
	Salt and freshly ground black pepper
4	¾-inch-thick lamb chops
1	cup bread crumbs
½	cup freshly grated Parmigiano
4	large eggs
½	cup milk
12 to 16	artichoke hearts, steamed until tender
1	cup olive oil
4	lemon wedges

Combine the first 6 ingredients in a pan just large enough to fit the lamb chops. Marinate the chops at room temperature for 4 hours, turning them once.

While the lamb is marinating, prepare the artichokes.

In a shallow pan mix together the bread crumbs, cheese, salt and pepper.

In a bowl, beat together the eggs, milk, salt and pepper.

Dip the artichokes in the egg wash, allowing the excess egg to drip off, then roll them in the bread crumbs.

Heat the oil in a skillet and fry the artichokes until they are golden all over. Drain on paper towels and keep them warm.

Place the lamb chops and the marinade in a shallow pan. Broil the lamb chops to the desired doneness, turning them once.

Transfer the chops to a warm serving dish and pour the marinade over them. Serve with the fried artichokes and lemon wedges.

LOMBATA DI MAIALE

Roast Loin of Pork with Zinfandel Sauce

SERVES 8 TO 10

1	4- or 5-pound pork loin, boned
	Salt and freshly ground black pepper
8	thin slices esrom
8	thin slices prosciutto
3	garlic cloves, finely chopped
2	cups coarsely chopped watercress (bottom stems removed)
3	garlic cloves, crushed
¾	cup olive oil or rendered pork fat
1	cup veal stock (page 50)

SAUCE

8	tablespoons butter
2	carrots, coarsely chopped
1	large onion, coarsely chopped
¼	cup red Zinfandel wine
¼	teaspoon dried thyme
1	cup seedless red grapes, coarsely chopped

Preheat the oven to 325 degrees.

Cut the loin in half lengthwise. Season both halves with salt and pepper. Sprinkle the chopped garlic on one of the halves, lay the slices of esrom over the garlic, lay the prosciutto over the cheese and spread the watercress over the prosciutto. Take the other half of the loin, seasoned side down, and lay it on top of the watercress. Tie the two halves securely together with string. Rub the outside of the tied loin with the crushed garlic and more salt and pepper.

Heat the oil in a large skillet and brown the loin on all sides. Remove the loin from the skillet and place it in a roasting pan. Add the veal stock to the pan and place it in the preheated oven. Roast the pork for 20 minutes per pound, basting it occasionally.

About 20 minutes before the meat has finished cooking, prepare the sauce. Melt the butter in a skillet. Add the carrots and onion and sauté until the vegetables are tender. Strain ¼ cup of the stock and drippings from the roasting pan and add it to the skillet with the vegetables. Add the Zinfandel and the thyme and let reduce for about 5 minutes.

Strain this sauce into another pan and add the grapes. Cook over low heat for about 5 minutes. Adjust the seasoning if necessary and keep warm.

Once the pork loin has finished cooking, remove it from the oven and let it sit for 5 minutes. Slice the pork and serve it with the sauce and additional sprigs of watercress.

ROGNONI TRIFOLATI
Veal Kidneys Sautéed with Prosciutto and Red Wine Vinegar

SERVES 4

4   veal kidneys
4   tablespoons red wine vinegar
4   tablespoons olive oil
1   cup thinly sliced onion
4   thin slices prosciutto, fat removed and cut into small pieces
½   cup red wine vinegar
2   teaspoons chopped fresh basil leaves
½   teaspoon dried marjoram
     Salt and freshly ground black pepper

Skin the kidneys and remove all tubes and fat. Cut the kidneys into ½-inch cubes. Immerse them in cold water to which you have added the 4 tablespoons vinegar and some salt. Let soak for 1 hour, then drain and rinse the kidneys, and pat them dry.

Heat the oil in a skillet or rondo and sauté the onion until it is brown and glazed. Add the prosciutto and kidneys. Lower the heat and cook for 2 minutes, stirring. Add the remaining ingredients and continue to simmer until the kidneys are cooked (not pink but still tender).

Serve the kidneys with the sauce spooned over them.

CONIGLIO ALLA MODENESE

Braised Rabbit with Porcini Sauce

SERVES 4

MARINADE

½ cup extra virgin olive oil
1 onion, chopped
2 carrots, chopped
2 celery stalks, chopped
6 ounces prosciutto, sliced and cut into ¼-inch pieces
½ cup red wine vinegar
3 cups dry white wine
6 fresh sage leaves
2 bay leaves
⅛ teaspoon chopped fresh rosemary leaves
2 garlic cloves
½ teaspoon whole black peppercorns
   Salt
2 rabbits, dressed and quartered

TO COOK

½ cup olive oil
¼ pound butter
4 tablespoons tomato paste
2 cups dry sherry
2 ounces dried porcini mushrooms
1 garlic clove, finely chopped
   Salt and freshly ground black pepper
   Fresh parsley and arugula for garnish

Make the marinade the night before.

Heat the oil in a saucepan. Add the vegetables and half of the prosciutto and sauté until tender. Add the vinegar, wine, herbs and spices and bring to a boil. Lower the heat and simmer for 10 minutes. Remove from the heat and let cool.

Place the rabbit pieces in a pan and pour the marinade over them. Cover and marinate at room temperature for 8 to 10 hours.

Remove the rabbit from the marinade and pat the pieces dry. Heat the oil and half of the butter in a large heavy skillet. Brown the rabbit pieces on all sides. Add the remaining prosciutto and cook slowly for 10 minutes.

Strain the marinade and add it to the skillet. Stir in the tomato paste and sherry. Cover the pan, lower the heat and cook slowly for 45 minutes.

While the rabbit is cooking, soak the mushrooms in 2 cups of tepid water for 40 minutes. Drain and rinse the mushrooms well, and pat them dry.

Heat the remaining butter in a skillet. Add the garlic and sauté for 30 seconds. Add the mushrooms, season with salt and pepper, and sauté for 2 minutes.

Arrange the rabbit on a warm serving platter. Remove the pieces of prosciutto from the pan and sprinkle them over the rabbit. Then arrange the mushrooms over and around the rabbit. Pour the sauce from the pan over all. Garnish with sprigs of fresh parsley and arugula.

UOVA

Eggs

Karl Knaths liked very much to give his opinion on artists. He said that Milton Avery was a better painter than Hans Hofmann, and when asked what he thought about Picasso, he replied, "He's a son-of-a-gun with shapes." One day Karl passed Ciro on the street and said out of the blue, "I'd like to give you a drawing of mine." He did not say why, and Ciro didn't think anything of it. A week later, a drawing arrived with a note attached thanking Ciro for all the meals he had given to Knaths.

◆————————◆

FRITTATA
Italian Omelet

SERVES 1

2 to 3	tablespoons olive oil or clarified butter (page 223)
	Salt and freshly ground black pepper
1	teaspoon finely chopped fresh parsley
1	small garlic clove, finely chopped
1	teaspoon finely chopped shallots
3	large eggs
	Freshly grated Parmigiano

In a bowl beat the eggs, salt, pepper and parsley together.

Heat the oil in an omelet pan. Add the garlic and shallots and sauté for 30 seconds over high heat. Add the eggs. As the eggs set, lift

160

the sides of the frittata so that the uncooked egg will flow under and cook. When almost all of the egg is cooked, either add the filling, or if it is to be a plain omelet, continue to the final step.

Place a plate over the pan and flip the frittata over onto the plate. Slide the frittata back into the pan and cook for 1 minute longer. Sprinkle with Parmigiano and serve immediately. The frittata is not folded in half as with the French omelet; instead, it is served as a flat circle.

An alternative to flipping the frittata is to place it 2 inches below a preheated broiler for 30 seconds.

Any range of fillings can be added to the frittata; your imagination is the limit. Here are some suggestions: sautéed zucchini; sautéed zucchini with fresh tomatoes and basil; fresh tomatoes, mozzarella and basil; Pecorino; thinly sliced sautéed potatoes and rosemary; prosciutto and sautéed mushrooms; shrimp and chives; sausage; sausage, roasted peppers and onions; black olives, goat cheese and fresh tomatoes; pancetta and potatoes; ricotta, fontina and Parmigiano. The possibilities are endless. These fillings may be mixed in with the beaten eggs or layered on top while the frittata is still cooking on the first side.

The frittata may also be sliced into wedges and served with Ragù or Simple Tomato Sauce.

It can be served as a hot or cold antipasto. It is also excellent rolled inside a veal roast.

FRITTATA CON PASTA

Pasta Omelet

SERVES 4 TO 8

This is an excellent way to use leftover sauced or unsauced pasta. Of course, it may also be made with freshly cooked pasta.

10   large eggs
½   cup freshly grated Parmigiano
     Salt and freshly ground black pepper
2   tablespoons chopped fresh parsley leaves
1   pound pasta cooked al dente (Fettuccine, spaghetti, penne, fusilli, etc., work well.)
¼   cup olive oil
2   garlic cloves, chopped finely
     Extra sauce (optional)

Separate 4 of the eggs. Save the whites. Add the yolks to the remaining 6 eggs and beat well. Add the Parmigiano, salt and pepper, and parsley to the eggs and mix well.

Pour the egg mixture over the pasta. Toss well.

Beat the egg whites until stiff and fold them into the pasta.

Heat the oil in a large cast-iron skillet. Add the garlic and sauté briefly over high heat. Pour the pasta mixture into the pan and smooth it into an even layer (it will probably be 2 inches thick). Cook over high heat for 10 minutes. Lower the heat and continue to cook for another 10 minutes.

If possible, place a large plate over the pan and flip the frittata over onto the plate. Slide the frittata back into the pan. Raise the heat and cook until the egg is set (about 15 minutes). The outside should be crispy. The frittata may also be baked in a hot (400-degree) oven if flipping is unmanageable.

Remove the frittata from the pan, slice it into wedges, and serve with extra sauce. If it was plain pasta (unsauced), use a sauce of your choice (the tomato-based sauces work best). If using plain pasta, some sauce may also be added to the pasta before frying. You should vary the seasonings according to your tastes. Fresh herbs work wonderfully.

This may be served as an antipasto, first course or light main course.

ZUCCHINI CON UOVA E FORMAGGIO
Zucchini with Eggs and Cheese

SERVES 4

4   *tablespoons olive oil*
½   *cup finely chopped onion*
4   *small zucchini, cut into thin rounds*
½   *cup chicken stock (page 51)*
4   *large eggs*
¼   *cup freshly grated Parmigiano*
    Salt and freshly ground black pepper
2   *tablespoons chopped fresh chives*

Heat the oil in a skillet. Add the onion and sauté until it is golden and glazed. Add the zucchini, stir and cook for 5 minutes. Add the chicken stock and salt and pepper to taste. Cook until the zucchini is *al dente*.

In a bowl, beat together the eggs, cheese, salt and pepper.

Remove the pan with the zucchini from the heat. Pour the egg mixture into the pan and stir well to set the eggs. Serve garnished with the chives.

UOVA LESSATE
Hard-Boiled Eggs with Olive Oil

SERVES 4

This may be served as an antipasto or light main course.

8   large eggs
4   tablespoons extra virgin olive oil
    Salt and freshly ground black pepper
8   anchovy fillets (optional)

Hard-boil the eggs, being careful not to overcook; the yolks should be yellow, not gray. (See Glossary.)

Peel the eggs and slice them in half lengthwise. Sprinkle the oil over them and season with salt and pepper. If desired, rinse the anchovy fillets, dry them well and drape them over the eggs.

Serve immediately with good crusty bread and perhaps a green salad and cheese.

UOVA AL PIATTO CON PATATE E PROSCIUTTO
Eggs Baked with Potatoes, Mozzarella and Prosciutto

SERVES 6

    Butter
6   small red or white potatoes
6   thin slices prosciutto
½   pound mozzarella, thinly sliced
6   large eggs
    Salt and freshly ground black pepper
    About 2 tablespoons grated Parmigiano
2   teaspoons of butter

Preheat the oven to 400 degrees.

Butter the inside of a baking dish large enough to hold 6 eggs without crowding them.

Boil the potatoes until they are tender, then peel and cut them into thin slices.

Layer the potatoes over the bottom of the baking dish. Layer the slices of prosciutto over the potatoes, and then layer the mozzarella over the prosciutto. Crack the eggs into the pan, keeping them evenly spaced. (You will have a whole egg on top of the layers of potato, prosciutto and cheese.) Season with salt and pepper and sprinkle with the grated cheese. Cut 2 teaspoons of butter into small pieces and distribute it over the eggs.

Bake for a few minutes, or until the whites of the eggs have set. Serve immediately.

UOVA AL PIATTO CON PROSCIUTTO E GRUVIERA

Eggs Baked with Prosciutto and Gruyère

SERVES 6

Butter
6   large eggs
6   thin slices prosciutto, cut into ¼-inch-wide strips
     Salt and freshly ground black pepper
3   ounces Gruyère, grated
2   tablespoons freshly grated Parmigiano
4   teaspoons butter, melted

Preheat the oven to 400 degrees.

Butter a baking dish. Break the eggs into it, keeping them separate. Arrange the strips of prosciutto around the yolks. Sprinkle with the Gruyère and then the Parmigiano and dribble the melted butter over all. Bake for a few minutes, or until the whites of the eggs have set. Serve immediately.

UOVA AL PIATTO ALLA TOSCANA
Eggs Baked with Spinach and Balsamella

SERVES 6

2	pounds fresh spinach, leaves only
4	tablespoons butter
½	medium-size onion, finely chopped
6 to 12	tablespoons grated Parmigiano
	Salt and freshly ground black pepper
	Pinch of freshly grated nutmeg
6	large eggs
1	cup Balsamella (page 192)

Wash the spinach leaves and place them in a large saucepan. Cover the pan and cook the spinach, without additional water, over low heat until it has wilted. Drain the spinach and squeeze out any excess liquid. Chop the spinach finely.

Preheat the oven to 350 degrees.

Melt the butter in a skillet and add the onion. Sauté until it is translucent. Add the spinach. Stir and sauté for another minute. Remove from the heat and season with salt, pepper and nutmeg. Then mix in 6 to 8 tablespoons of the Parmigiano.

Butter a round baking dish. Arrange the spinach in a ring along the outer edge of the dish. Break the eggs into the center of the bowl, keeping them separate. Cover the eggs with the Balsamella. Sprinkle with the remaining Parmigiano and bake for about 15 minutes, or until the whites of the eggs are set. Serve immediately.

NOTE: This can also be done in individual ceramic dishes. A variation would be to use a Tomato Balsamella (page 192).

UOVA SODE E FRITTE

Hard-Boiled Eggs Stuffed with Ricotta and Fried

6 SERVINGS

6	hard-boiled large eggs, peeled and cut in half lengthwise
¾	cup whole milk ricotta
1	heaping tablespoon grated Parmigiano
	Pinch of ground nutmeg
	Salt and freshly ground black pepper
½	cup (approximately) all-purpose flour, seasoned with salt and pepper
1	large egg, beaten and seasoned with salt and pepper
½	cup (approximately) dry bread crumbs
¼	teaspoon dried oregano
½	teaspoon dried basil
1½	cups olive oil

Remove the yolks from the eggs and mix them well with the ricotta, Parmigiano, nutmeg and salt and pepper to taste. Stuff the mixture back into the cavities where the yolks had been and over the white of the egg also. You should have a smooth mound over the cut surface of the egg. (It will be almost the size of a whole egg again.) Once you have done this with all the eggs, roll each very carefully in the flour. (Pat back into shape with a knife, if necessary.) Then dip each in the beaten egg and roll them very gently in the bread crumbs which have been seasoned with the oregano and basil, being careful to cover them completely.

Heat the oil in a skillet with high sides. (Do not let the oil smoke.) Fry the eggs until they are a deep golden color. Drain on paper towels and serve immediately.

ORTAGGI E LEGUMI

Vegetables

I have always loved Italian food, music and art, but it wasn't until I received a Fulbright and an Italian government grant to go to Italy with my wife and two children for a year that I really began to understand the Italian culture.

I returned with my family another year, on my own to do bronze casting, and then by myself on several more trips. So in the past twenty years I have spent about two and a half years in Rome in the artists' quarter, Trastevere.

One of the things I began to notice about Italian cooking was that all my Italian friends, whether they had yards or just balconies, grew fresh basil as well as other herbs and spices. I think the average Italian would give up anything rather than his fresh basil.

On one of the many occasions that Ciro was generously donating his time, food, money and backyard for a fund raiser for the Art Association I noticed an amazing growth of basil. It was about two to three feet tall and looked almost like a hedge around the entire lawn. When I asked Ciro about it he said, "Sure, I always grow my own fresh herbs for the restaurant!" This is typical of how Ciro insists on the best food for his restaurant.

—JACK KEARNEY

◆————————◆

CUORI DI CARCIOFI ROMANELLI

Artichoke Hearts Broiled with Prosciutto and Parmigiano

SERVES 4 TO 5

20	artichoke hearts
½	lemon
3	tablespoons clarified butter (page 223)
2	garlic cloves, finely chopped
¼	cup dry white wine
	Juice of ½ lemon
	Freshly ground black pepper
4	thin slices of prosciutto, trimmed of excess fat
1½	tablespoons bread crumbs, seasoned with salt and pepper
1½	tablespoons freshly grated Parmigiano

Preheat the broiler.

Bring 2 quarts of water to a boil. Add some salt and the juice of ½ lemon to it. Put the artichokes into the water and cook until tender but not soft (al dente). Drain the artichokes and plunge them into ice cold water. When they are cold, drain them well.

Heat the butter in a skillet. Add the garlic and sauté until it is golden. Add the artichokes, wine, lemon juice and black pepper. Cook the artichokes for about 7 minutes, stirring occasionally.

Transfer the artichokes to an ovenproof dish. Arrange the slices of prosciutto over the artichokes. Combine the bread crumbs and grated cheese and sprinkle the mixture over the prosciutto.

Place the pan under the broiler and broil just until the bread crumb and cheese mixture is browned.

FAGIOLI AL FIASCO
Beans in a Bottle
SERVES 4

Traditionally these beans were cooked in a bottle, but they can be cooked in a heavy casserole with equally good results. The beans are excellent with good crusty bread and wine for a simple meal. They can also be spread on Bruschette (page 33) for a simple meal or as an antipasto.

1   *pound dried cannellini beans, sorted and rinsed*
½   *cup extra virgin olive oil*
3   *garlic cloves, pressed*
4 to 5 *fresh sage leaves, stems removed*
       Salt and freshly ground black pepper

Soak the beans overnight in cold water to cover. Drain and put them into a heavy 2-quart casserole. Add the oil, garlic and sage. Pour in enough water to cover the beans by 1 inch.

Cover the pan tightly and set it over very low heat. Let the beans cook for about 2 hours, by which time almost all of the water and oil will be absorbed.

Transfer the beans to a warm bowl. Season with salt and pepper and toss carefully.

NOTE: Another variation is to add 2 to 4 tablespoons of red wine vinegar to the warm beans for more of a marinated salad.

FAGIOLINI CON PROSCIUTTO
String Beans with Prosciutto
SERVES 6

1½ *pounds young tender string beans*
4   *tablespoons butter*
6   *thin slices prosciutto, excess fat removed*
    Salt and freshly ground black pepper

Remove the stems from the beans. Blanch the beans in salted water. Drain them and cool them in ice water. Drain again and dry the beans well.

Melt the butter in a heavy skillet. Add the beans and toss to coat them with the butter and sauté for 3 minutes.

Cut the prosciutto into ¼-inch squares and add it to the beans. Season with salt and pepper. Stir and sauté the beans over moderate heat until they are tender.

BROCCOLI AL CRUDO *excellent*
Broccoli Sautéed with Oil, Garlic and Lemon

SERVES 4

1   bunch fresh broccoli
¼   cup olive oil
2   garlic cloves, finely chopped
    Juice of ½ lemon
2   tablespoons dry white wine
    Salt and freshly ground black pepper
    Lemon slices or wedges for garnish

Cut off the tough ends of the broccoli stems. Peel the stems to remove the tough skin. Blanch the broccoli in a small amount of boiling salted water; then plunge into ice cold water and drain well. Cut the broccoli into small spears, keeping the spears of equal size.

Heat the oil in a skillet. Add the garlic and sauté until it is golden, then add the broccoli and the remaining ingredients. Cover the pan and cook over low heat until the broccoli is tender but not soft (*al dente*). Transfer the broccoli to a warm serving dish and pour the pan juices over it. Garnish with lemon slices and serve immediately.

BROCCOLI CON AGLIO E OLIO
Broccoli Sautéed with Garlic and Oil

SERVES 4 TO 6

1	bunch fresh broccoli
2	tablespoons extra virgin olive oil
3	garlic cloves, thinly sliced
2	tablespoons dry white wine
	Salt and freshly ground black pepper
8 to 10	black olives, sliced thinly lengthwise (optional)
2 to 4	ounces soft Pecorino or goat cheese (optional)
	Lemon wedges for garnish

Cut off the tough ends of the broccoli stems. Peel the stems to remove the tough skin. Divide the broccoli into small spears of equal size.

Blanch the broccoli in boiling salted water. Then plunge the broccoli into ice cold water to chill it, and drain well.

Heat the olive oil in a skillet. Add the garlic and sauté it over low heat until it is golden. Discard the garlic. Add the broccoli to the skillet and toss to coat each spear with oil. Cook for 2 minutes over moderate heat. Add the wine, salt and pepper, raise the heat and let the wine reduce to about 2 tablespoons. Cover the pan and cook over low heat until the broccoli is tender.

If desired, the black olives and cheese may be added at the last moment. Serve immediately garnished with lemon wedges.

BROCCOLETTI CON AGLIO E OLIO
Broccoli Rabe Sautéed with Garlic and Oil

SERVES 4 TO 6

Broccoletti is often sold in the American markets under the name "broccoli rabe." It is a dark green leafy vegetable with a slightly bitter taste. This preparation brings out the sweetness of the greens.

1   *pound broccoletti*
¼   *cup extra virgin olive oil*
3   *garlic cloves, thinly sliced*
     Salt

Wash the broccoletti in cold water. Cut off the bottoms of the stems if they are bruised. Cut the broccoletti into 1-inch pieces, leaving some of the small leaves whole.

Heat the oil in a heavy skillet. Add the garlic and sauté until it is lightly browned, then discard the garlic.

Add the broccoletti to the pan and toss to coat it with the oil. Lower the heat, cover the pan and cook the broccoletti only until it has wilted. Add the salt and continue to cook, uncovered, until tender. Stir occasionally.

CAVOLINI DI BRUXELLES CON PIGNOLI
Brussels Sprouts with Pine Nuts

SERVES 6

2   *pounds brussels sprouts, with small compact heads*
½   *cup pine nuts*
4   *tablespoons butter*
     Salt and freshly ground black pepper

Remove the stems and outer leaves of the brussels sprouts. Cut an 'X' into the base of each sprout (this aids in the cooking).

Steam the sprouts until they are tender. Plunge the sprouts into ice water, then drain and dry them thoroughly.

Toast the pine nuts in a skillet over low heat until they are golden brown.

Melt the butter in a skillet, then add the brussels sprouts, pine nuts, and salt and pepper. Stir well and sauté for 3 minutes. Serve immediately.

CAVOLFIORE AL ROMANO

Cauliflower with Tomatoes and Parsley

SERVES 6

1	head cauliflower
¼ to ½	cup extra virgin olive oil
2	garlic cloves, peeled
2	parsley sprigs
2	plum tomatoes, peeled, seeded and finely chopped
	Salt

Remove the core and outer leaves from the cauliflower and separate it into 1- to 1½-inch flowerets.

Heat the oil in a heavy saucepan. Add the whole garlic cloves and
let them cook for 1 minute (be careful not to let them burn). Add the
cauliflower and the remaining ingredients to the pan. Lower the heat
and cook the cauliflower slowly until it is tender, stirring gently from
time to time.

Discard the garlic and parsley and serve immediately.

CAVOLO ALL' AGRO E DOLCE

Sweet and Sour Cabbage

SERVES 6

1	head red cabbage
4 to 6	tablespoons olive oil
1	garlic clove, crushed and peeled
2	tablespoons honey
¼	cup red wine vinegar
¼	cup water
	Salt and freshly ground black pepper

Remove the outer leaves from the cabbage. Cut it into quarters
and remove the core. Cut each quarter into ¼-inch-thick slices.

Heat the oil in a large skillet. Add the garlic and sauté until it is
golden, then remove and discard. Add the cabbage to the pan, cover
and cook over moderate heat until it is wilted.

Mix the honey, vinegar and water together and add the mixture to the cabbage. Season with salt and pepper, cover and cook until the cabbage is tender.

FINOCCHI ALLA PARMIGIANA
Fennel Sautéed with Butter and Parmigiano
SERVES 4 TO 6

2	*small heads fennel*
4 to 6	*tablespoons butter*
2	*tablespoons dry white wine*
	Salt and freshly ground black pepper
2	*ounces freshly grated Parmigiano*

Remove the tops from the fennel bulbs and save them to use in soups. Trim the base of the bulbs and remove any tough or bruised outside layers. Cut the fennel bulbs into 1-inch-thick slices. Do not use any of the feathery greens in the core.

Melt the butter in a skillet. Add the fennel and sauté for 5 minutes. Add the wine, salt and pepper and cook the fennel until tender. Sprinkle on the Parmigiano and serve immediately.

FUNGHI CON VINO
Mushrooms Sautéed with Garlic and White Wine
SERVES 4

4	*tablespoons clarified butter (page 223)*
2	*garlic cloves, finely chopped*
3	*cups fresh mushrooms, sliced or quartered*
½	*cup dry white wine*
4	*teaspoons finely chopped fresh parsley leaves*
	Salt and freshly ground black pepper

Heat the butter in a skillet. Add the garlic and sauté until it is golden, then remove the garlic and discard it. Add the mushrooms, parsley, salt and pepper to the pan. Stir and sauté for 3 minutes.

Add the wine and cook for another 3 minutes. Serve immediately.

FUNGHI AFFUMICATI

Smoked Mushrooms

SERVES 4 TO 6

This recipe was taught to me by my dear friend Genovina in Italy. The mushrooms are not actually smoked, but this is the name she gave me, so I shall use it here. They are delicious just the same.

1   *pound wild mushrooms*
¼   *cup extra virgin olive oil*
2   *garlic cloves, peeled*
1   *plum tomato, peeled, seeded and finely chopped*
2   *tablespoons dry white wine*
1   *parsley sprig*
      Salt

Remove any tough stems from the mushrooms and wash them quickly in cold water. Do not dry them.

Put the mushrooms in a heavy casserole pan with a little water over low heat. Cover and cook the mushrooms until they have expelled a good amount of liquid, 20 to 30 minutes. Discard the liquid.

Heat the oil in another heavy casserole. Add the whole garlic gloves, lower the heat and sauté the garlic for 1 minute. Add the mushrooms and remaining ingredients and cook slowly until the mushrooms are quite tender, about 20 minutes. Stir the mushrooms carefully from time to time.

Discard the garlic cloves and parsley and serve immediately.

PISELLI CON PROSCIUTTO

Peas Sautéed with Prosciutto and Onion

SERVES 4

1 cup chicken stock (page 51)
1 pound fresh peas (Thawed frozen peas can be substituted.)
3 tablespoons clarified butter (page 223)
¼ pound thinly sliced prosciutto, chopped
1 onion, finely chopped
Salt and freshly ground black pepper

Bring the chicken stock to a boil in a saucepan. Cook the peas in the stock until they are tender then drain the peas and save the stock for use in another dish.

Heat the butter in a skillet. Add the prosciutto and the onion and sauté until the onion is translucent.

Add the peas, salt and pepper and stir. Cook for 1 minute and serve immediately.

PATATE LESSATE

Boiled Potatoes with Olive Oil

Boil as many potatoes as you will need (usually 1 per person). When the potatoes are soft, remove them from the water and peel immediately. They may now either be mashed with a fork or riced (much prettier). Place on a warm serving plate and pour a generous amount of a good, extra virgin olive oil over the potatoes. Season with salt and pepper and serve immediately.

BIETOLE CON CIPOLLE E POMODORI
Swiss Chard Sautéed with Onion and Tomatoes

SERVES 6

2   pounds Swiss chard
¼   cup extra virgin olive oil
2   garlic cloves, peeled
1   onion, chopped or sliced thinly lengthwise
2   tablespoons dry white wine
6   plum tomatoes, peeled, seeded and finely chopped
   Salt and freshly ground black pepper

Wash the Swiss chard in cold water and dry thoroughly. Trim the bottoms of the stems. Separate the stems from the leafy tops and cut the stems thinly on the diagonal. Roll the leaves and slice them thinly along the width.

Heat the oil in a large skillet or saucepan. Add the whole garlic cloves and cook until they are golden, then remove and discard.

Add the Swiss chard and the onion to the pan. Toss rapidly to coat the Swiss chard with the oil. Cover the pan and cook over low heat for 5 to 10 minutes, or until the chard has wilted. Add the remaining ingredients, stir and cook until the Swiss chard is tender.

NOTE: The onion and tomato may be omitted if a simpler dish is desired.

POMODORI RIPIENI

Tomatoes Stuffed with Rice and Ricotta

SERVES 6

6	large ripe tomatoes
1	cup Arborio rice
¼	cup dry white wine
1¼	cups chicken stock (page 51)
	Salt
3	garlic cloves, finely chopped
2	shallots, finely chopped
2	tablespoons olive oil
¼	cup ricotta or shredded fresh mozzarella
2	ounces freshly grated Parmigiano
6	fresh basil leaves, chopped
	Freshly ground black pepper

Preheat the oven to 400 degrees.

Cut the tops off the tomatoes and set them aside. Carefully scoop out the seeds and pulp from the tomatoes. Pass the pulp through a sieve to remove the seeds and reserve.

Put the rice, wine, stock and tomato pulp in a saucepan. Add salt to taste. Bring to a boil and cook the rice, covered, until it is very *al dente* (remember that it will be cooked again later). If there is any excess liquid, drain it from the rice.

Remove the rice from the heat. Sauté the garlic and shallots in the olive oil for 2 minutes, then add them to the rice with the remaining ingredients and mix well.

Season the inside of the tomatoes with salt and pepper.

Fill each tomato with approximately ¼ cup of the rice mixture. Cover each tomato with its top.

Arrange the tomatoes in an oiled baking pan. Pour a little olive oil over the tomatoes. Cover the pan with aluminum foil and bake for approximately 20 to 30 minutes. Serve immediately.

ZUCCHINI CON BASILICO E POMODORI
Zucchini with Basil and Tomatoes
SERVES 6

This is a summer dish that should be made only with fresh basil and the freshest, ripest tomatoes.

6	small zucchini
⅛	cup extra virgin olive oil
2	garlic cloves, thinly sliced
2	tablespoons dry white wine
2	large ripe tomatoes, cored and cut into ½-inch wedges
	Salt
6	fresh basil leaves, stems removed

Wash and trim the ends off the zucchini, then slice it into thin rounds.

Heat the oil in a skillet. Add the garlic and sauté until it is golden brown, then remove and discard.

Add the zucchini to the pan and sauté for 5 minutes. Add the wine, tomatoes and salt. Stir gently and cook over moderate heat for 2 minutes. Add the basil leaves and cook until the zucchini is tender.

ZUCCHINI FRITTI

Fried Zucchini

SERVES 4

2   *medium-size zucchini*
2   *large eggs*
2   *tablespoons milk*
     Salt and freshly ground black pepper
½   *cup all-purpose flour*
2   *cups bread crumbs*
1   *cup vegetable oil*
4   *lemon wedges*

Wash and trim the ends off the zucchini, then cut it lengthwise into slices approximately ¼-inch thick. Discard the first and last slices.

Beat the eggs and milk together in a shallow pan. Season with salt and pepper. Place the flour in another shallow pan and season it with salt and pepper also. Do the same with the bread crumbs.

Submerge the zucchini slices in the beaten egg, then dredge them in the flour, shaking off any excess. Dip the slices once again in the beaten egg and then dredge them in the bread crumbs.

Heat the oil in a skillet and sauté the zucchini slices on both sides until golden brown. Remove them from the pan and drain them on paper towels.

Arrange the zucchini slices on a warm serving dish and garnish with the lemon wedges. Serve immediately.

ORTAGGI ARROSTI CON AIOLI

Roasted Vegetables with Garlic Mayonnaise

SERVES 4

1	*small eggplant (The Japanese variety works well.)*
1	*small yellow summer squash*
1	*small zucchini*
1	*small head fennel*
¼ to ½	*pound wild mushrooms*
½	*cup extra virgin olive oil*
1	*garlic clove, finely chopped*
1	*teaspoon fresh rosemary leaves, chopped*
	Salt and freshly ground black pepper
½	*cup Aioli (page 191)*

Preheat the grill.

Prepare the vegetables: Cut the ends off the eggplant, yellow squash and zucchini. Cut the vegetables into ½-inch wedges. Prepare the fennel as for the Finocchi alla Parmigiana (page 175), but do not cook it. Cut any tough stems off the mushrooms.

Combine all the remaining ingredients except the Aioli in a large bowl or pan. Add the vegetables and toss well to thoroughly coat them with the oil. Allow them to marinate for 30 minutes to 1 hour.

Grill the vegetables, turning them once, until they are tender, approximately 2 minutes on each side.

Arrange the vegetables on a large platter and place the Aioli in the center as a dipping sauce or drizzle it over them.

NOTE: An alternate method is to braise the vegetables. Simply add ¼ cup of chicken stock and ¼ cup of dry white wine to the marinade. Place the vegetables with the marinade in a roasting pan. Cover the pan and cook in a 400 degree oven until the vegetables are tender.

Remove the vegetables from the braising liquid and arrange them as you would for the roasted vegetables.

INSALATE

Salads

INSALATA DI PENNE CON
TONNO E BROCCOLI

Pasta Salad with Tuna and Broccoli

SERVES 4

1	bunch fresh broccoli
1	pound white tuna or swordfish
1	pound penne
4	ripe tomatoes, cored and cut into thin wedges
1	pound fresh mozzarella, cut into ¼-inch cubes
8	black olives, cut into thin slivers
½	cup walnuts, toasted
4	garlic cloves, finely chopped
2	tablespoons chopped fresh parsley leaves
	Salt and freshly ground black pepper
4	anchovy fillets, rinsed and dried
¾	cup extra virgin olive oil

Put a large pot of salted water on to boil for the penne.

Separate all the broccoli flowerets from the stalks. Save the stalks for another use. The flowerets should be uniform in size (about 1 inch in diameter). Blanch the broccoli in the pasta water. When it is *al dente*, remove it from the water, transfer it to a bowl of ice water and drain thoroughly.

If the tuna or swordfish is fresh, poach it in a little water with white wine and lemon juice. Let the fish cool and then break it into small chunks.

Cook the penne in the salted boiling water until they are *al dente*. Drain and rinse under cold running water until completely cooled, then drain completely.

Put the penne in a large serving bowl. Add all the remaining ingredients, except the anchovies and olive oil.

Heat the olive oil in a small pan over low heat. Cut the anchovy fillets into small pieces, add them to the olive oil and mash them with a fork until they dissolve. Do not let the oil get too hot. Pour the oil-anchovy mixture over the salad. Toss very well and serve immediately.

INSALATA DI FUSILLI CON FRUTTI DI MARE
Pasta Salad with Seafood
SERVES 4

½	pound shrimp, shelled and deveined
½	pound squid, cleaned and cut into rings
3	tablespoons dry white wine
¼	lemon
16	littleneck clams, washed
1	pound fusilli
1 to 1½	cups cold Puttanesca Sauce (see recipe for Spaghetti alla Puttanesca, page 61)
¼	cup extra virgin olive oil
2	tablespoons finely chopped fresh parsley leaves
	Salt and freshly ground black pepper

Poach the shrimp and squid in a little water with the white wine and lemon juice. Once they are tender, remove them from the pan and shock them in ice water and drain completely.

Steam the clams until they open. Let them cool and remove them from their shells.

Cook the fusilli in salted boiling water until it is *al dente*. Drain and cool completely under cold running water, then drain again.

Put the fusilli in a large bowl. Cut the shrimp in half through the back; if they are large, cut the two sides in half again. Add the shrimp, squid and clams to the fusilli.

Blend the Puttanesca Sauce, oil and parsley in a food processor until smooth.

Add the sauce to the salad and toss well. Season with salt and pepper and serve immediately.

INSALATA DI ARAGOSTA E CONCHIGLIE

Lobster and Scallop Salad with Basil-Ginger Mayonnaise

SERVES 4

1	*pound lobster meat, cooked*
½	*pound sea scallops*
2	*tablespoons dry white wine*
¼	*lemon*
1	*cup Maionese (page 191)*
1	*garlic clove, finely chopped*
2	*teaspoons grated fresh ginger*
8	*fresh basil leaves, chopped*
1	*teaspoon fresh lemon juice*
	Salt
	Bibb or Boston lettuce leaves

Cut the lobster meat into ½-inch pieces. Poach the scallops in a little water with the white wine and lemon juice. Cool the scallops completely. If they are large, cut them in half.

Blend all the remaining ingredients except the lettuce leaves in a food processor.

Add the Maionese dressing to the lobster and scallops and toss very well. Serve on lettuce leaves.

NOTE: This also makes an excellent cold pasta salad. Simply add it to a pound of cooked fusilli.

INSALATA DI LENTICHIE
Lentil Salad with Balsamic Vinegar and Mustard
SERVES 6

1	tablespoon shallots, finely chopped
1	teaspoon garlic, finely chopped
1	tablespoon Dijon mustard
1 to 1½	tablespoons balsamic vinegar
2	teaspoons cream sherry
2	teaspoons dry vermouth
¼	cup extra virgin olive oil
	Salt and freshly ground black pepper
1	recipe for Minestra di Lentichie (page 44)

Mix together the first 6 ingredients in a large bowl. Slowly whisk in the oil and season with salt and pepper.

Drain the cooked lentils, add them to the marinade while they are still hot and toss well. Let the lentils marinate for 30 minutes before serving.

INSALATA MISTA
Spinach and Arugula Salad
SERVES 4 TO 6

1	pound spinach, leaves only
1	large handful arugula leaves
1	Belgian endive
8	fresh mushrooms
	Juice of ½ lemon
¼	cup extra virgin olive oil
	Salt and freshly ground black pepper

Wash the spinach and arugula and dry the leaves completely. Thinly slice the endive leaves on the diagonal. Thinly slice the mushrooms. Toss all the vegetables together in a large serving bowl.

Whisk together the lemon juice, olive oil, salt and pepper. Pour the dressing over the salad and toss well. Serve immediately.

INSALATA DI RADICCHIO E CANNELLINI
Radicchio and Cannellini Bean Salad

SERVES 4

1	garlic clove, finely chopped
2	tablespoons red wine vinegar
¼	cup extra virgin olive oil
	Salt and freshly ground black pepper
2	small heads radicchio
½	recipe for Fagioli al Fiasco (page 171—this must be started the night before)

Prepare the cannellini beans; you will have to start the night before.

Whisk together the garlic, vinegar, oil, salt and pepper. Let the dressing sit for 30 minutes.

Separate all the leaves of the radicchio and tear them into 2-inch pieces. (An alternative is to roll the leaves and slice them thickly across the width.)

Combine the beans and radicchio and toss well. Whisk the dressing, pour it over the salad and toss well. Serve immediately.

INSALATA DI POMODORO, BASILICO E MOZZARELLA
Tomato, Basil and Mozzarella Salad

Simply cut a pound of fresh mozzarella into ½-inch cubes and add them to the marinating tomatoes (recipe for Insalata di Pomodoro e Basilico) for the last 15 minutes.

Another option is to slice the mozzarella and tomatoes into rounds and arrange them in overlapping layers of mozzarella, tomato and basil leaf. Pour the marinade over the center of the arrangement.

INSALATA DI POMODORO E BASILICO
Tomato and Basil Salad

SERVES 4

As with all salads, only the freshest seasonal ingredients should be used. Therefore, this is a salad for the summer when fresh garden tomatoes and basil are abundant.

4   *large ripe tomatoes, cored and cut into ¾-inch wedges*
2   *garlic cloves, finely chopped*
4   *whole basil leaves, stems removed*
½   *cup extra virgin olive oil*
     Salt

Combine all the ingredients in a bowl. Toss well but gently. Let the salad marinate at room temperature for 1 hour. Serve accompanied by good crusty bread.

INSALATA ALLA NAPOLITANA
Neopolitan Salad of Tomatoes, Basil and Red Onion

SERVES 4

4   *large ripe tomatoes, cored and cut into ¾-inch wedges*
1   *small red onion, cut into thin rounds*
4   *whole basil leaves*
2   *garlic cloves, finely chopped*
½   *cup extra virgin olive oil*
1½   *teaspoons dried oregano*
     Salt and freshly ground black pepper

Combine all the ingredients and toss well but gently. Let marinate at room temperature for 1 hour.

SALSE
Salad Dressings and Sauces

*H*ans Hofmann *always complained that there was not enough color in the dishes.*

NOTE: Interesting dressings can be made by adding various flavorings to a simple oil and vinegar mixture (2 parts oil to 1 part vinegar). Try adding mustard, fresh herbs, chopped scallions, shallots or garlic. Use flavored vinegars (tarragon vinegar for example). Whip Maionese or Aioli into any of the dressings below. Experiment, and if you are timid about putting two flavors together, try them in small amounts to see how they taste.

SALSA DI ACETO E OLIO
Salad Dressing
MAKES 4 CUPS

1   cup red wine vinegar
1¼ tablespoons finely chopped garlic
1½ tablespoons dried basil
1½ teaspoons dried oregano
2   teaspoons salt
1   teaspoon freshly ground black pepper
3   cups olive oil

Whisk together all the ingredients or blend in a food processor or blender.

MAIONESE
Mayonnaise

6 *large egg yolks*
1 *tablespoon fresh lemon juice*
2 *cups extra virgin olive oil, or a lighter olive oil if you prefer a*
   lighter Maionese
   Salt

Put the eggs in a food processor and blend the yolks. Keep the machine running and add the lemon juice, then add the oil very slowly. Once all the oil is added, season with salt. The Maionese will be very thick. If a thinner sauce is desired, a little water may be blended into the Maionese.

If you add the oil too quickly and the Maionese breaks (becomes liquid), it can be saved. Remove the broken sauce from the processor. Place 2 more egg yolks in the processor and while blending, very slowly pour the broken sauce into the processor. This should get you what you're looking for.

AIOLI
Garlic Mayonnaise

Add 2-4 cloves, finely chopped garlic (depending on your love of garlic) to the Maionese and blend.

MAIONESE
Use your imagination with Maionese and Aioli to make very interesting dressings. Here are some suggestions to get you going:

Add fresh herbs (basil, rosemary, tarragon, parsley)
Add saffron or curry
Substitute vinegar for the lemon juice
Use extra vinegar or a flavored vinegar
Add extra lemon juice
Add capers and anchovies
Add roasted sweet red peppers

BALSAMELLA

Besciamel Sauce

MAKES 2 CUPS

4 *tablespoons butter*
4 *tablespoons all-purpose flour*
1 *cup milk*
1 *cup light cream*
   Pinch of nutmeg
1 *bay leaf*
   Salt and freshly ground white pepper

Melt the butter in a saucepan without letting it brown. Slowly whisk in the flour. Cook for 2 minutes over low heat, stirring constantly.

Combine the milk and cream in another saucepan and heat it just to the boiling point. Do not let it come to a boil.

Slowly add the milk to the butter-flour mixture, whisking constantly. Add the nutmeg, bay leaf, salt and pepper. Continue to cook the sauce over low heat, stirring constantly, for 5 minutes.

If the sauce is not to be used immediately, lightly butter one side of a piece of wax paper and place it over the surface of the sauce (it should touch the sauce). This will prevent a skin from forming.

BALSAMELLA

This, like Maionese, can have many variations. Try adding:

Tomato paste
Sautéed onions
Sautéed mushrooms (sliced or chopped)
Fresh herbs
Blanched julienned vegetables
Puréed vegetables

SALSA PICCANTE
Piquant Sauce

MAKES ABOUT ¼ CUP

This is a Neapolitan sauce to which I have added a little Pommerey mustard. If you are a traditionalist, leave out the mustard. This sauce is excellent on fish cooked in any fashion or with boiled meats.

1	medium-size onion, finely chopped
⅔	cup Giardinera (page 28)
2	tablespoons capers, rinsed and drained
6	gherkins (not the sweet kind)
3	parsley sprigs (leaves only)
1	thyme sprig, or ½ teaspoon dried thyme
½	cup extra virgin olive oil
1	teaspoon Pommerey mustard
	Juice of ½ lemon
	Salt and freshly ground black pepper

Finely chop together the first 6 ingredients. Put the mixture in a heavy-bottomed saucepan, cover and simmer over low heat for 1½ to 2 hours, or until all the ingredients are soft.

Pass the mixture through a sieve and return it to the pan. Add the remaining ingredients and cook over very low heat for 10 minutes more.

SALSA VERDE

Green Sauce

MAKES ½ TO ¾ CUP

This sauce is delicious on fish. It can also be added to Maionese (page 191) and used as a dressing for cold fish dishes or seafood salads.

¼   cup fresh bread crumbs
2   tablespoons red wine vinegar
¼   cup extra virgin olive oil
10 anchovy fillets
2   hard-boiled egg yolks
    Juice of ½ lemon
½   cup fresh basil leaves (no stems)
½   cup fresh parsley leaves
    Freshly ground black pepper

Soak the bread crumbs in the vinegar for about 5 minutes. Squeeze any excess vinegar from the crumbs (use your hands to do this). Combine the bread crumbs with the remaining ingredients and blend in a food processor until smooth. Do not blend too long if you prefer a sauce with more texture.

NOTE: This sauce can be varied in several ways: 1) for a more piquant sauce, add 2 tablespoons of capers and one large clove of garlic, 2) add four leaves of fresh mint, 3) substitute tuna for the hard-boiled eggs or for half of the anchovies, 4) do all of the above.

ESPAGNOLE SAUCE

Brown Sauce

MAKES 1 QUART

We use this sauce often in our preparation of meats and in certain meat-based stuffed pastas.

3	pounds veal bones
1	ham bone
1	large onion, stuck with 3 whole cloves
½	cup clarified butter (page 223)
3	garlic cloves, peeled and crushed
4	carrots, peeled and chopped coarsely
3	celery stalks, chopped coarsely
½	cup all-purpose flour
3	cups dry white wine
2	tablespoons tomato paste
3	quarts water
1	teaspoon whole black peppercorns, crushed
3	bay leaves
½	teaspoon dried thyme
5	parsley sprigs

Preheat the oven to 475 degrees.

Put the bones and the onion in a roasting pan. Brown the bones in the oven for 30 minutes, turning them occasionally.

Heat the butter in a saucepan and add the garlic, carrots and celery. Sauté over low heat for 10 minutes. Add the flour and stir for another 5 minutes. Stir in the wine and tomato paste. Raise the heat and bring the wine to a boil. Add all the remaining ingredients and bring the sauce to a boil once again.

Add the sauce to the roasting pan with the bones and onion and return the pan to the oven. Lower the oven temperature to 275 degrees. Let the sauce cook for 5 hours, stirring occasionally.

Remove the sauce from the oven and allow it to cool. Strain the sauce through a medium mesh strainer and discard the solids. The sauce can be frozen in small amounts for later use, or it can be tightly sealed and refrigerated for several days.

PANE E PIZZE

Bread and Pizza

N orman Mailer said he always ordered Médoc wine "because Redon liked it." Over the years, the hostesses at both of Ciro's restaurants in Provincetown have had to be very careful never to seat Norman next to any of his ex-wives.

◆————————◆

FOCACCIA

SERVES ABOUT 10

This is a flat bread that is actually like a pizza without the topping. The Italians eat it as a snack, either as is, or sliced in half with some thin slices of prosciutto between.

SPONGE
1	package active dry yeast, or ½ ounce (1 cake) fresh compressed yeast
	Pinch of sugar
¾	cup tepid water
¾	cup unbleached white flour

DOUGH
1	tablespoon coarsely chopped fresh rosemary, or sage leaves (optional)
2	teaspoons salt
3	tablespoons olive oil
1	cup unbleached white flour

196

TOPPING

2   tablespoons extra virgin olive oil or whole rosemary or sage
           leaves or coarse salt

Make the sponge: In a large mixing bowl, dissolve the yeast and sugar in the water. Let the yeast sit until it begins to foam (this means that it is alive and working). Mix in the ¾ cup of flour and beat in an up and down circular motion (i.e., the down stroke goes through the center of the dough, and the up stroke comes up the side of the bowl). This stroke will help incorporate air into the dough. Using a wooden spoon, beat for 200 strokes. Cover the bowl tightly and set it in a warm (80 to 85 degree) place. Let the sponge rise until doubled, about 1 hour.

Stir down the sponge and add the fresh herbs, salt and olive oil. (If you wish, omit the herbs and top the focaccia with coarse salt before baking.) Stir to blend. Add the flour and mix to get a smooth, soft dough. Turn the dough out onto a lightly floured board and knead it vigorously for about 8 minutes, or until it is smooth and elastic.

Lightly oil the inside of a large mixing bowl. Form the dough into a ball and roll it around the inside of the bowl so that it is lightly coated with oil. Cover the bowl tightly and set it in a warm place. Let the dough rise until doubled, about 1 hour.

Line the shelf of your oven with unglazed quarry (ceramic) tiles (available at tile stores) and preheat it to 500 degrees (it will take about 30 minutes). The tiles will hold the heat and are important to the baking process. Lightly flour a baking sheet.

Punch the dough down and roll it out into an oblong or rectangular shape, ¼- to ⅛-inch thick. Lay the dough on the baking sheet. Sprinkle the remaining olive oil over the surface of the dough and spread it over the entire surface with your fingertips. Sprinkle with either the fresh herbs or the coarse salt.

Bake for about 15 minutes, or until golden brown. The focaccia is best eaten immediately.

GRISSINI

Very Thin Breadsticks

MAKES 35 TO 40 BREADSTICKS

⅔   cup tepid water
1   package active dry yeast, or ½ ounce (1 cake) fresh compressed
        yeast
4   tablespoons olive oil
1   teaspoon salt
1½ cup unbleached white flour
¼   cup cornmeal
1   tablespoon crushed fennel seeds or chopped rosemary or sage
        leaves

In a large mixing bowl, dissolve the yeast in the water and let sit until it begins to foam (5 to 10 minutes). Add the oil and salt to the yeast and stir to mix. Add 2 cups of the flour and beat with a wooden spoon for 100 strokes. Beat the dough using a vertical circular motion.

Add the seeds or herbs, the remaining flour and the cornmeal. Mix thoroughly to get a soft dough that does not stick to the sides of the bowl. If the dough is sticky, add a little more flour.

Turn the dough out onto a lightly floured board and knead vigorously for 5 to 8 minutes, or until the dough is smooth and elastic. Test its elasticity by pressing your thumb into the dough ball. If the identation springs back, it is ready.

Lightly oil the inside of a bowl large enough to accommodate the dough once it has doubled in size. Form the dough into a ball and roll it around the inside of the bowl so that it is lightly coated with oil. Cover the bowl tightly and set it in a warm place (80 to 85 degrees). Let the dough rise until doubled, about 1 hour.

Grease a large baking sheet.

Punch the dough down with your fist and turn it out onto a lightly floured board. Knead it for 30 seconds. Pull off half-dollar-size balls (the dough should yield about 35 or 40). Using the outstretched palms of your hands, roll out each piece until it is long and very thin (thinner than a pencil). They will not all be perfectly shaped. Lay the sticks on the baking sheet, leaving ½ inch between them. Once all the sticks have been rolled out (or as many as you can fit on the baking sheet), let them rest for 30 minutes.

While the dough is resting, preheat the oven to 325 degrees.

Place the baking sheet in the oven and bake the breadsticks until they are golden brown, 15 to 30 minutes.

Remove the breadsticks from the oven and let cool. Store them tightly wrapped in a cool, dry place or freeze in plastic wrap and aluminum foil.

PANE

Bread

MAKES 2 LOAVES

This recipe makes two round, crusty, yeast-flavored loaves. This bread must be started at least a day in advance.

STARTER

1	package active dry yeast, or ½ ounce (1 cake) fresh compressed yeast
1	cup tepid water
½	cup whole wheat or rye flour
½	cup unbleached white flour

SPONGE

2	cups tepid water
3	cups unbleached white flour

DOUGH

1	tablespoon salt
2	tablespoons olive oil
3½ to 4	cups unbleached white flour.

In a large mixing bowl (preferably a ceramic bread bowl), dissolve the yeast in the water. Let it sit until it becomes foamy. Add the flour and beat until smooth (use a wooden spoon). Cover the bowl tightly and set in a warm place (80 to 85 degrees) for 1 day. During this time, the mixture will bubble and expand and develop a strong yeasty odor.

The next day, make the sponge. Add the water to the yeast mixture and stir to mix. Add the flour and beat for 200 strokes in an up and down circular motion. Cover the bowl and set it in a warm place.

If an especially yeasty flavor is desired, let the sponge sit for 1 day; otherwise, let the sponge rise until doubled in size, about 1 to 2 hours.

Stir the sponge down and add the salt and olive oil. Stir to mix. Add the flour ½ cup at a time, mixing well after each addition, until you have a soft dough that no longer sticks to the sides of the bowl. Turn the dough out onto a floured board and knead vigorously for 10 to 12 minutes, or until the dough is smooth and elastic (sprinkle the board and the dough with flour as necessary to keep the dough from sticking).

Lightly oil the inside of a large mixing bowl. Form the dough into a ball and roll it around the inside of the bowl so that the dough is coated lightly with oil. Cover the bowl tightly and set it in a warm place. Let the dough rise until doubled, about 1 hour.

Punch down the dough and divide it in half. Form each half into a ball. Lightly flour 2 kitchen towels on one side. Set each ball of dough on the floured side and wrap the towel around the dough. Let the dough rise for 30 minutes or until doubled.

While the dough is rising, line the oven shelf with unglazed quarry (ceramic) tiles and preheat it to 425 degrees (this will take 20 to 30 minutes). Lightly oil a baking sheet.

Transfer the loaves to the baking sheet, and using a razor blade or a very sharp knife, make 4 shallow slashes to form a square on the top of each loaf.

Bake the loaves for 40 to 50 minutes. To test for doneness, tap the bottom of each loaf. It will sound hollow when it is cooked.

Let the loaves cool completely on wire racks before slicing.

NOTE: These loaves also freeze well, wrapped in plastic wrap and aluminum foil.

PIZZA

This recipe makes one thin-crust pizza about 12 to 14 inches in diameter.

DOUGH

1	*package active dry yeast or ½ ounce (1 cake) fresh compressed yeast*
½	*cup tepid water*
1½	*cups unbleached white flour*
3	*tablespoons extra virgin olive oil*
1	*teaspoon salt*

TOPPING

10	*anchovy fillets*
½ to ¾	*cup (about 8 ounces) mozzarella, cut in small cubes or shredded*
12	*ounces Italian plum tomatoes, peeled, seeded and chopped*
	Pinch oregano
	Salt and freshly ground black pepper

In a small bowl, dissolve the yeast in the water. Let stand until it begins to foam.

Sift the flour into a large mixing bowl and make a well in the center. Add the yeast mixture, 1 tablespoon of the olive oil and the salt to the well, and slowly incorporate them into the flour (use a wooden spoon). The dough should be soft and should not stick to the sides of the bowl (add more flour if necessary).

Turn the dough out onto a lightly floured board and knead it vigorously for 6 to 8 minutes or until the dough is smooth and elastic. Lightly oil a mixing bowl (preferably ceramic). Form the dough into a ball and place it in the bowl. Roll the dough around so that it becomes lightly coated with oil. Cover the bowl tightly and set it in a warm place (80 to 85 degrees). Let the dough rise until it doubles, about 1 to 2 hours.

Line the oven shelf with unglazed quarry (ceramic) tiles and preheat it to 500 degrees. Lightly oil a 14-inch pizza pan or a terracotta pan.

Punch the dough down and turn it out onto a lightly floured board. Knead it for 30 seconds. Using your hands (this takes practice), flatten the dough and stretch it out into a circle (or rectangle, depending on your pan). Place the dough in the pan and push it with your fingers to fit the pan. Beat down the dough with your outstretched hand until it is ⅛- to ¼-inch thick and fits the pan. If the dough extends over the sides of the pan, tuck it under itself to form an edge.

Sprinkle 1 to 1½ tablespoons of olive oil over the dough and smooth it over the entire surface. Arrange the anchovies, mozzarella and tomatoes over the surface (or use any of the toppings listed below). Leave a plain border about ½-inch wide. Sprinkle on the oregano, salt, pepper and remaining olive oil.

Bake for 20 to 30 minutes or until the crust is golden and crispy.

OTHER TOPPINGS:

Sautéed onions
Raw whole egg (place it in the center of the pizza)
Hard-boiled eggs, sliced thinly or chopped
Sautéed peppers, mushrooms, etc.
Sautéed eggplant
Pre-soaked porcini mushrooms
Pre-soaked sun-dried tomatoes
Provolone, Pecorino, ricotta, Parmigiano, goat cheese
Prosciutto, salami or sausage
Chopped raw clams seasoned with fresh parsley and oregano
Fresh basil and fresh tomatoes
Tuna
Capers

PIZZA FRITTA

Fried Dough

SERVES 4 TO 6

1	cup water
2	tablespoons olive oil
1	teaspoon salt
1	teaspoon sugar
2	teaspoons active dry yeast
3	cups all-purpose flour
4	cups vegetable oil
	Granulated sugar or honey

Combine the water, olive oil, salt and sugar in a small saucepan and heat until lukewarm. Remove from the heat and add the yeast. Stir to dissolve the yeast and let stand for 5 to 10 minutes (if the yeast is active, it should be foamy by this time).

Sift the flour into a mixing bowl. Make a well in the flour and pour the yeast mixture into the well, slowly mixing the flour into the liquid. Once all or almost all of the flour has been used, turn the dough out onto a lightly floured board and knead for 3 to 4 minutes, or until it is smooth and elastic.

Place the dough in a lightly oiled bowl, cover it tightly, and set it to rise in a warm place for 1 to 2 hours, or until doubled in bulk.

Punch down the dough, turn it out onto a lightly floured surface and divide it into 10 or 20 pieces (depending on what size you desire). Form each piece into either balls or flattened circles.

Let the pizze (doughs) rest while you heat the oil in a deep skillet. Use a piece of one of the dough balls to test the temperature of the oil—it should fall to the bottom and then rise quickly to the surface.

Have paper towels ready for draining the pizze. Heat the oven to keep the pizze warm once they have been cooked.

Fry the pizze a few at a time (they should have space around them in the pan). Fry them until golden on one side, then flip them over and cook until golden on the second side. Remove them from the oil with a slotted spoon and set them to drain on the paper towels. Then keep them warm on a heat-resistant plate in the oven.

Once all of the pizze have been fried, sprinkle them with granulated sugar or drizzle honey over them and serve immediately.

If you want to have these for breakfast, the dough may be left to rise in the refrigerator overnight. The next morning you can divide the dough and let it come to room temperature. Fry the pizze and serve with the sugar or honey.

NOTE: These pizze can also be served as a light lunch or dinner. Follow the directions for preparing the pizze but instead of the sugar or honey, place on each pizza a spoonful of the sauce from the Penne all' Arrabiata recipe. Sprinkle with freshly grated Pecorino and place in a hot oven until the cheese melts. Serve immediately.

DOLCI

Desserts

During the first years of the restaurant, the desserts were mostly fresh fruit. Because Ciro and Sal did not have a liquor license, they put spirits in the desserts—peaches in red wine, pears in port, figs in brandy.

Ciro's wife Ero wanted to create a dessert that was luscious but still refreshing, as fruit is after a heavy Italian meal. After some experimentation, she created a pie that combined the creaminess of ice cream, the crunchiness of graham crackers and the tartness of lime. It was an instant success and has remained the most requested dessert on the menu for over thirty years. Steady customers still call in advance to make sure the lime pie is on the menu and will even go so far as to reserve a piece as extra insurance.

Artist Leo Manso says he recalls "with nostalgia and pleasure Ciro's 'Family Table.'

"The old pine table flanked by equally ancient benches on both sides (probably from the town dump), stood near the doors to the kitchen and was reserved for staff, friends and artists—an underground artistocracy. It was not very comfortable, the ambience was noisy and busy as hell, with artist-waiters continually going in and out of the kitchen, a constant ferment of activity.

"Nevertheless, you always enjoyed sitting there—better than sitting on those little barrels with no backs, which hardened your rump while you devoured your pasta.

"At any rate, while waiting for your order, you were constantly tantalized by the odors of Pasta Carbonara, Puttanesca, alle Vongole, etc., as the orders were carried from the kitchen to the patrons. By the time your order arrived, your taste buds had devoured all that passing food. The pasta was magnificent, and finally that great lime pie!

"Not only that, Ciro generously poured you a brandy on the house!"

LA DOLCE VITA
The Sweet Life

SERVES 6 TO 8

1   pound cake or an equal amount of ladyfingers
2   large very ripe peaches
½   of a fresh pineapple
2   large very ripe pears
1   pound fresh strawberries
2   cups vanilla pudding (page 212)
       Ground cinnamon
       Whipped cream

Cut the pound cake into ½-inch-thick slices or split the lady-fingers. Line the bottom of a deep serving dish with the cake slices. slices.

Peel and seed the peaches and pears, and cut them into bite-size chunks. Cut the rind off of the pineapple and remove the core. Cut the flesh into bite-size chunks. Hull the strawberries and slice them in half.

Arrange one third of all the fruit over the first layer of cake. Cover the fruit with one third of the pudding. Sprinkle with cinnamon. Cover this with a layer of the cake slices and repeat the process until you have made a third layer and used all of the ingredients. Refrigerate for 1 hour.

Serve in individual dessert glasses and top with softly whipped cream.

CASSATA ALLA SICILIANA

Pound Cake with Sweetened Ricotta and Chocolate

SERVES 8

4	*ounces semisweet chocolate*
12	*tablespoons sweet butter*
½	*cup brewed Espresso (Italian coffee)*
1	*pound ricotta*
¼	*cup confectioner's sugar*
¼	*cup mixed candied citrus peel*
¼	*cup semisweet chocolate shavings*
1	*pound cake (page 220)*
¼	*cup Triple Sec*

To make the frosting melt the 4 ounces of semisweet chocolate and the butter together in the top of a double boiler over simmering water. Stir to mix and then whisk in the Espresso. Remove the chocolate mixture from the heat and place it in the refrigerator. Stir every 15 minutes until it is smooth and firm.

Mix together the ricotta, sugar and candied citrus peels. Beat until smooth, then fold in the chocolate shavings.

Cut the pound cake twice lengthwise, creating 3 layers.

Sprinkle half of the Triple Sec on the bottom layer. Spread half of the ricotta mixture on the pound cake (if you are using homemade, be sure that it is completely cooled). Top with the second layer and repeat the process. Top with the third and final layer.

Cover the entire cake with ¼ inch of frosting. To do this, use a narrow cake spatula dipped occasionally in hot water.

Serve at room temperature. This cake keeps well in the refrigerator.

ZUPPA INGLESE
Sponge Cake Layered with Rum and Zabaione
SERVES 8 TO 12

2   sponge cake layers (page 221)
1½   cups dark rum
½   recipe for Zabaione (page 209)
12   large egg whites (Use the yolks to make the Zabaione.)
½   cup confectioner's sugar

Peheat the oven to 400 degrees.

Split each sponge cake layer in half to make 4 layers in all.

Place the first layer on an ovenproof serving dish and sprinkle it with one third of the rum. Spread one third of the Zabaione over the layer. Repeat with the second and third layers. Top with the fourth layer.

Beat the egg whites, slowly adding the sugar, until they are stiff. Cover the cake entirely with the meringue, forming decorative peaks and swirls.

Bake the cake just until the meringue is browned.

CANNOLI
Pastry Shells Filled with Sweetened Ricotta
SERVES 6

1   pound whole milk ricotta (2 cups)
¼   cup confectioner's sugar
¼   cup mixed candied fruit
2   tablespoons crème de cacao
¼   cup semisweet chocolate shavings
6   cannoli shells (may be purchased at Italian pastry shops or
        specialty stores)

Beat the ricotta, sugar, candied fruit, and crème de cacao together until smooth and light. Fold in the chocolate.

Fill the shells with the ricotta mixture. Arrange them on a serving dish and dust them with more confectioner's sugar. Serve immediately.

ZABAIONE

Marsala and Cream Custard

SERVES 6

6   large egg yolks
¼   cup sugar
1   cup Marsala
1½   cups heavy cream
      Slivered almonds for garnish

Put the egg yolks and sugar in the top of a double boiler. Beat with a whisk until they are light yellow. (Do not heat.)

Bring water in the bottom of the double boiler to a boil, then lower the heat so that the water only simmers. Add the Marsala to the eggs and put the top of the double boiler over the simmering water. Stir constantly with a whisk or wooden spoon until the mixture coats the spoon. Be careful not to overcook. Remove from the heat and let cool completely.

Whip the cream and fold it into the cooled mixture.

Pour the zabaione into stemmed glasses and refrigerate for 1 hour. Serve with a sprinkle of slivered almonds.

CUORE DI PANNA

Heart of Cream

SERVES 6

12   ounces cream cheese, at room temperature
¾   cup confectioner's sugar
1½   teaspoons vanilla extract
3   cups heavy cream
1½   cups fresh strawberries, halved

Beat the cream cheese, sugar and vanilla together until light and fluffy.

Whip the heavy cream separately (it should be stiff), then fold the whipped cream into the cream cheese mixture.

Line 6 heart-shaped porcelain molds (they must have perforated bottoms) with cheesecloth.

Fill the molds with the cream mixture and smooth out the tops. Refrigerate for 3 to 4 hours.

To serve, unmold the hearts onto cold serving plates and sprinkle with the fresh strawberries.

ZUCCOTTO

Frozen Layers of Flavored Whipped Cream

SERVES 10

1   pound cake (page 220)
¼   cup Triple Sec
3   cups heavy or whipping cream
1   tablespoon brandy
1½   ounces semisweet chocolate, melted and cooled
1   teaspoon vanilla extract
1   teaspoon confectioner's sugar
¼   cup mixed candied citrus peels
⅓   cup finely chopped fresh strawberries

Cut the pound cake into ⅜-inch-thick slices. Cut each of these slices on the diagonal to get two triangles. Moisten each triangle with a sprinkle of the Triple Sec.

Line a 2-quart round-bottomed bowl with the slices of cake. Start at the bottom of the bowl and work up the sides, covering the entire inside of the bowl.

Whip 1 cup of the cream, the brandy and the chocolate until stiff. Pour the whipped cream into the cake-lined bowl and smooth it into a flat surface. Freeze the bowl until the cream has hardened.

Whip the second cup of cream, the vanilla and the sugar until stiff. Fold in the candied citrus peels. Put this over the frozen layer of chocolate whipped cream. Smooth the surface and freeze until hardened.

Whip the third cup of cream until stiff and fold in the strawberries. Pour it over the second frozen layer. Smooth the surface and freeze until hardened.

When ready to serve, dip the bottom of the bowl in hot water for an instant. Place a cold flat dish over the top of the bowl and invert. The cake will fall out onto the dish. It should be a perfect dome.

Cut the cake into wedges and serve on chilled plates.

SUFFLÈ AL CIOCCOLATO
Chocolate Mousse

SERVES 4 TO 6

8   *ounces semisweet chocolate*
3   *teaspoons brewed coffee*
6   *large eggs, separated*
4   *teaspoons dark rum or cognac*
⅓   *cup sugar*

Put the chocolate and coffee in the top of a double boiler. Heating over simmering water until the chocolate has melted, then remove from the heat. Add the egg yolks and rum or cognac and blend until smooth. Let cool.

Beat the egg whites until stiff, adding the sugar slowly. Fold the beaten whites into the chocolate mixture.

Spoon the mousse into stemmed glasses and refrigerate for 1 hour.

To serve, top with whipped cream and chocolate shavings, or whipped cream and grated orange rind, or both.

VANILLA PUDDING

MAKES 3 CUPS

5	*large egg yolks*
½	*cup sugar*
2	*cups milk or light cream*
1	*teaspoon vanilla extract*

In a mixing bowl, whisk together the eggs and sugar until they are light and foamy.

Scald the milk or cream. Remove it from the heat and gradually whisk it into the egg and sugar mixture.

Pour this mixture into a heavy-bottomed saucepan and place it over moderate heat. Heat just to the point before boiling, being careful not to let it boil. Lower the heat and continue to cook, stirring constantly with a wooden spoon, until the mixture coats the spoon. Remove from the heat.

Stir in the vanilla and keep stirring until the mixture cools. If you do not want to use the pudding immediately, butter one side of a piece of wax paper and place it over the surface of the pudding. Refrigerate until needed.

NOTE: Various flavorings can be added to the pudding if desired: Substitute almond extract for the vanilla (use ¼ teaspoon); add grated orange or lemon rinds to the pudding while it is cooking; mix in toasted, chopped hazelnuts, walnuts or almonds.

CROSTATA ALLA MARMELLATA
Marmalade Tart

SERVES 8

1¾	*cups unbleached white flour*
½	*cup sugar*
8	*tablespoons sweet butter, at room temperature*
½	*teaspoon grated lemon rind*
1	*large egg yolk*

2 to 3   *tablespoons heavy cream*
12   *ounces (about 1 cup) marmalade (peach, apricot and*
            raspberry work well)
1   *teaspoon Triple Sec*

Lightly butter the bottom of a 9-inch tart pan with a removable bottom.

Mix together the flour and sugar. Cut the butter into small pieces and add it to the flour. Quickly mix the butter into the flour. (The flour will have a sandlike texture when the butter is properly incorporated.)

Mix the lemon rind into the flour, then make a well in the mixture and add the egg yolk. Slowly incorporate the egg into the flour mixture. Now do the same with the cream. Use only enough cream to hold the dough together.

Form the dough into a ball, place it on a lightly floured surface and roll it out into a ¼-inch-thick circle. Fit the dough into the tart pan. The sides should be almost ½-inch-thick, and there should be no excess dough. Refrigerate the tart shell for 1 hour.

In the meantime, preheat the oven to 400 degrees. Prepare the marmalade. Add the Triple Sec or liqueur of your choice to the marmalade. Heat it slowly and stir until smooth. Remove from the heat and set aside.

Remove the tart shell from the refrigerator. Cover it with aluminum foil or parchment or wax paper, weight it down with dried beans or rice and bake the crust for 20 minutes. Remove the beans and foil and return the crust to the oven for another 20 minutes.

Remove the tart shell from the oven and spread the marmalade over the center. If the edges are very brown, cover them with foil. Return the tart to the oven for 10 minutes.

Remove the crostata from the oven and let it cool slightly before removing it from the tart form.

CROSTATA DI MELE

Apple Tart

SERVES 8

1¾	cups unbleached white flour
½	cup sugar
8	tablespoons sweet butter, at room temperature
½	teaspoon grated lemon rind
1	large egg yolk
2 to 3	tablespoons heavy cream
6	tablespoons apricot jam
2	tablespoons water
3	large Granny Smith apples
2	tablespoons dark brown sugar
1	tablespoon brandy

Prepare the crust as for the Crostata alla Marmellata up to the first baking.

Preheat the oven to 400 degrees.

Mix together the jam and water in a saucepan. Bring to a boil and cook for 3 minutes. Let cool.

Peel and core the apples. Cut each in half and slice each half into ¼-inch-thick slices. Toss the slices in the sugar and sprinkle with the brandy.

Brush the inside bottom of the tart with a thin layer of the jam. Arrange the apple slices in the tart shell. Brush with more of the jam if you want more of a glaze.

Bake the crostata for 45 minutes.

Fresh, very ripe peaches may be substituted for the apples. Bake the tart shell as for the Crostata alla Marmellata. After approximately 40 minutes of baking, remove the shell from the oven and brush the inside with a little marmalade. Arrange the peach slices in the shell and brush them with a little of the marmalade. Bake the tart 10 minutes longer.

BISCOTTI SEMPLICI
Plain Biscuits

MAKES 40 TO 45 BISCOTTI

These are excellent with coffee or tea.

6   *large eggs, separated*
1¼   *cups sugar*
2   *tablespoons liqueur of your choice (Amaretto or anisette are
       excellent.)*
2   *cups unbleached flour*
1½   *teaspoons baking powder*
¼   *cup walnuts or almonds, coarsely chopped*

Preheat the oven to 400 degrees.

Lightly butter the bottom and sides of a 9-inch springform pan. Line the bottom with buttered parchment, or wax paper.

Beat the egg yolks well and add the sugar. Continue beating until the mixture becomes light yellow, then add the liqueur and mix it in.

In a separate bowl, beat the egg whites until they form soft peaks. Fold the egg whites into the egg yolk mixture. Add the flour and the baking powder a little at a time, and beat until the batter becomes smooth and light, about 2 minutes.

Sprinkle half of the chopped nuts over the bottom of the spring-form pan. Pour in the batter and sprinkle the remaining nuts over the top.

Bake for 20 to 25 minutes. The cake should be golden and slightly springy. Remove the cake from the oven and let it cool on a wire rack.

Heat the oven to 450 degrees. When the cake is completely cooled, slice it horizontally to create 2 layers. Cut each layer into 2- by 1-inch rectangles.

Place the rectangles on an unbuttered baking sheet, leaving a space between them. Bake the biscotti until they are a rich brown color. Turn them so all the sides brown evenly. When they are done cooking they will still feel a little springy but will harden as they cool.

PARFAIT GELATO

Ice Cream Pie

SERVES 16

½   gallon vanilla ice cream
1   cup lime-flavored gelatin powder
¾   cup fresh lemon juice
12   tablespoons sweet butter
3½   cups plain graham cracker crumbs
     Whipped cream
     Grated rind of 1 lime

Let the ice cream sit at room temperature until it has softened (not melted) (about 30 minutes).

Combine the gelatin powder and the lemon juice in a saucepan, bring to a boil and stir to dissolve the powder. Remove the mixture from the heat and let it cool.

Melt the butter in a skillet and add the graham cracker crumbs. Stir well to thoroughly combine the graham cracker crumbs and the butter. Place half of this mixture in each of two 9-inch-round pie plates. Using a large spoon, press the crumb mixture into the pie form. The mixture should evenly cover the bottom and sides.

Beat the gelatin-lemon juice mixture together with the ice cream until fluffy. Pour half of this into each pie form. Refrigerate the pies until they have set completely. Serve garnished with the whipped cream and grated lime rind.

Here are some additional flavors that can be substituted for lime:

LEMON: Follow the basic recipe, substituting lemon-flavored gelatine for the lime.

FRUIT: Follow the basic recipe, substituting lemon-flavored gelatin for the lime and using only ½ cup of lemon juice. Coarsely chop strawberries, peaches or pineapple and fold them into the pie mixture after the ice cream.

MOCHA RUM: Follow the basic recipe, substituting lemon-flavored gelatin for the lime. Use ½ cup of brewed coffee, to which a teaspoon of instant coffee has been added, instead of the lemon juice. Substitute chocolate ice cream for the vanilla and add 3 tablespoons of rum to the ice cream.

COFFEE-BRANDY: Substitute lemon-flavored gelatin for the lime and ½ cup brewed coffee for the lemon juice. Substitute coffee ice cream for the vanilla and add 3 tablespoons of brandy to the ice cream.

LADYFINGERS

MAKES 100

3 large eggs
2 large egg yolks
¾ cup granulated sugar
1¼ cups unbleached white flour, sifted
¼ teaspoon grated lemon rind

Preheat the oven to 400 degrees. Line a baking sheet with ungreased wax paper.

Bring a small amount of water to a boil in a medium-size saucepan. In a stainless steel mixing bowl, whisk together the eggs, egg yolks and sugar. Place this bowl over the boiling water and lower the heat so that the water barely simmers. Cook the mixture, stirring constantly with a wooden spoon, until it forms a soft foam and a spoonful of the batter poured back into the bowl forms a "ribbon" (maintains some of its shape before dissolving).

Remove the bowl from the heat and stir the mixture until it is almost cold. Fold in the sifted flour and grated lemon rind.

Fill a pastry tube with the dough and squeeze finger lengths onto the prepared sheet, leaving ½ inch between each finger. Bake for about 15 minutes.

NOTE: These freeze well when tightly wrapped in a plastic wrap.

CIAMBELLA

Sweet Bread

MAKES 1 LOAF

This is a moist, cakelike bread that is excellent with rich Italian coffee.

1	cup milk
1	teaspoon honey
1	teaspoon active dry yeast
2	large eggs
4	teaspoons olive oil
3¾	cups unbleached white flour
½	cup sugar
	Pinch of salt
2 to 3	teaspoons anise seeds

Heat the milk until it is tepid. Stir the honey into the milk, then sprinkle the yeast into the milk and stir well to dissolve. Let stand for 5 to 10 minutes, or until the yeast is foamy (this means it is active).

Beat the eggs and add them to the milk, then add the oil.

Mix together the flour, sugar, salt and anise. Make a well in the flour and pour in the milk mixture. Using a wooden spoon, mix everything together and continue mixing in an up and down circular motion for 200 strokes.

Cover the bowl tightly with plastic wrap and let it sit, away from drafts, overnight at room temperature (68 degrees).

The next morning beat down the dough with a wooden spoon or your hand. Do this by turning the dough in on itself several times, adding a little more of the flour if it is very sticky.

Turn the dough out on a lightly floured board. You will find that the dough is already quite elastic, so knead it lightly for only 2 minutes. Roll the dough into a thick log shape and form it into a ring. Join the edges well.

Lightly butter a baking sheet and place the dough ring on it. Set the dough in a warm place and allow it to rise for 20 to 30 minutes.

While the dough is rising, preheat the oven to 400 degrees.

Bake the bread for 30 to 40 minutes. It will be golden colored and quite springy to the touch. Tap the bottom; it will have a hollow sound when it is done. Near the end of the baking period, brush the loaf with milk to give it a sheen.

Let the bread cool completely on a wire rack before slicing.

POUND CAKE

MAKES 3–4 CAKES

I can't remember where I found this recipe, but I have used it over the years to make a delicious, rich pound cake.

1   *pound sweet butter*
3   *cups granulated sugar*
6   *large eggs*
1   *cup milk or light cream*
2   *teaspoons vanilla extract*
1   *tablespoon baking powder*
4   *cups unbleached white flour*

Preheat the oven to 350 degrees. Butter and flour two 9- by 4- by 2-inch loaf pans.

Cream together the butter and sugar until light and fluffy. Add the eggs one at a time and beat well after each addition.

Sift together the flour and baking powder. In a separate bowl, mix together the milk and the vanilla. Add small amounts of the flour and milk mixtures to the butter mixture alternately, beginning and ending with the flour. Use a wooden spoon to blend after each addition. You do not need to beat this.

Pour the batter into the prepared loaf pans. Bake for about 40 minutes. The top should be golden, and a toothpick inserted in the center should come out dry.

Let the cakes cool in the pans for 10 minutes, then remove them from the pans and let them cool completely on wire racks.

NOTE: This cake freezes well when tightly wrapped in plastic wrap and aluminum foil.

SPONGE CAKE

MAKES 2 CAKES

10 large eggs
1¼ cups granulated sugar
½ teaspoon vanilla
1 cup unbleached white flour
1 cup cornstarch
7 tablespoons sweet butter, melted

Preheat the oven to 425 degrees.

Butter two 10-inch-round layer pans or a sheet cake pan. Line each with wax paper.

Bring a small amount of water to a boil in a medium-size saucepan. Whisk together the eggs, sugar and vanilla in a stainless steel mixing bowl. Place the bowl over the boiling water and lower the heat so that the water simmers slowly. Cook, stirring constantly with a wooden spoon, until the batter forms a soft foam and draws into a ribbon.

Remove the bowl from the heat and continue to stir until the batter is almost cool.

Sift together the flour and cornstarch and fold it into the batter, then fold in the melted butter.

Pour the batter into the pans and bake for 25 to 30 minutes. Turn off the oven and prop open the oven door. Leave the cakes in the oven for 5 minutes more.

Remove from the oven. Turn the cakes out of the pans, let cool on wire racks and cool completely before slicing.

GELATO ALLA CREMA

Cream Flavored Ice Cream

SERVES 6

5   large egg yolks
⅔   cup sugar
2   cups milk
2   teaspoons vanilla extract

Beat the egg yolks with a whisk in the top of a double boiler or a mixing bowl large enough to fit over a pan of boiling water. Add the sugar and beat until the mixture becomes a very light yellow.

In a separate saucepan, bring the milk just to the boiling point, but do not let it boil.

Place the bowl with the egg-sugar mixture over a saucepan of boiling water. Lower the heat so that the water simmers slowly.

Add the warm milk little by little to the eggs, whisking the milk completely into the eggs after each addition. Add the vanilla and continue cooking the mixture, stirring continuously with a wooden spoon until the mixture thickens slightly. When it is done, it should be the consistency of thin pudding and should coat the spoon. Be very careful not to overcook it, as the eggs will harden.

Remove the bowl from the heat and set it in the refrigerator to cool. Stir occasionally to facilitate the cooling. Once it is cool, transfer the mixture to a loaf pan.

Place the pan in the freezer and stir the gelato every 30 minutes for 2 hours. The finished gelato will be thick, smooth and soft. It should be served in smaller quantities than American ice cream, because it is quite dense.

GLOSSARY OF INGREDIENTS AND COOKING TECHNIQUES

Anchovies (Acciughe)

Buy anchovy fillets that are packed in olive oil, preferably an imported brand. Store any unused anchovies in their own oil, tightly wrapped in the refrigerator.

If you can find them, the whole, salt-packed anchovies are excellent. Wash off all the salt and bone the anchovies. To do so, slice down the belly and lift out the bone. You will be left with two fillets. Store any unused fillets in olive oil in the refrigerator. They will become too strongly flavored after 2 or 3 days, so use them immediately.

Bread Crumbs (Pangrattato)

To grate fresh bread crumbs, remove the crusts from slices of fresh Italian bread and rub the bread into the palm of your hand. This will crumble the bread sufficiently.

For dried bread crumbs, use stale bread and grate it in a food processor or blender until it is fairly fine. If you do not have any stale bread on hand, you can simply dry out slices of bread in a warm oven.

Butter (Burro)

In the recipes, I call for "butter" and "clarified butter." By butter I mean butter that has not been clarified. For baking, I always use sweet butter, but for cooking, lightly salted butter may be used.

I often specify to use clarified butter because it has a much higher burning point than whole butter (i.e., it can withstand higher temperatures); however, whole butter may be used instead of clarified if you are careful not to let it burn.

To clarify butter, melt at least 2 pounds of sweet butter in a heavy-bottomed saucepan. Once it has melted, you will be left with three layers: The top is a layer of white, foamy milk solids; the middle is the clarified butter; the bottom is water. Skim off the milk solids with a ladle and discard them. Ladle out the butter, being careful not to mix it with the water, and reserve it in a small saucepan. Throw away the water. This clarified butter may be stored tightly covered in the refrigerator and reheated as needed.

223

Cheese (Formaggio)

Cheese should be bought in small quantities that can be consumed within a few days. Always serve cheese at room temperature. Store any extra cheese tightly wrapped in plastic wrap and aluminum foil in the refrigerator; if the cheese will be eaten within two days, it can be tightly wrapped and left out of the refrigerator in a cool place. It is best to buy grating cheeses in small chunks and to grate them by hand as needed. Keep the chunks tightly wrapped in a cool, dry place. If a large quantity is needed, grate only the necessary amount.

Asiago: A delicately flavored cheese from Vicenza that is made from either whole or skimmed cow's milk. It has small holes throughout and is excellent as a table or a cooking cheese. The aged asiago is used for grating.

Bel Paese: A soft, mild cheese made from cow's milk. It is excellent both as a table cheese and as a cooking cheese.

Caciocavallo: A cow's milk cheese from Southern Italy. It is shaped like a sack and has a stringy (layered) texture. The semi-hard table cheese is delicate and sweet, while the hard grating cheese is sharp and robust.

Caciotta di pecora: A semi-hard, sweet cheese that is made from sheep's milk. It comes from both Sardegna and Central Italy and is good both as a table and a cooking cheese.

Caciotta: A soft cheese from central Italy. It is made from cow's milk and has a sweeter flavor than the caciotta made from sheep's milk.

Emmental: A cow's milk cheese from Switzerland. It is a semi-hard cheese with large holes and is sweet and flavorful. It is used both as a table and a cooking cheese.

Fior di Latte Treccia: A stringy, soft cheese much like mozzarella but made from cow's milk. It is slightly less flavorful than the mozzarella and is sold in braids. Store as you would mozzarella.

Fontina: A cow's milk cheese from Val d'Aosta. It is a semi-hard cheese with a sweet, delicate flavor. It is excellent both as a table cheese and as a cooking cheese.

Gorgonzola: A cow's milk cheese from Lombardy and Piedmont that is characterized by blue mold spores (much like blue cheese or roquefort). The soft Gorgonzola is mild and is excellent both as a table cheese and as a cooking cheese. The harder cheese is much more piquant and is excellent for the table.

Gruyère: Another Swiss cheese made from cow's milk but with a stronger flavor than emmental. It is a harder cheese that is often used in cooking, but it also makes an excellent table cheese.

Mascarpone: A very soft, buttery cheese with a sweet, delicate flavor. It is used in cooking and in desserts, as well as being an excellent table cheese.

Mozzarella di bufala: A stringy, soft cheese from Southern Italy. It is made from water buffalo's milk and has a sweet, slightly acidic flavor. It is excellent both as a table cheese and as a cooking cheese. It should be stored wrapped in paper in a bowl of water in the refrigerator. It will keep only a couple of days. It is available in small and large balls.

The mozzarella typically found in U.S. supermarkets is made from cow's milk. It is a harder cheese that is used in cooking or as the standard topping for pizza.

Mozzarella affumicata: Same as mozzarella but smoked.

Parmigiano-Reggiano: This is a hard cheese made from partially skimmed cow's milk. The yellower type is more delicate and is better as a table cheese, while the whiter version is better for grating. The grated Parmigiano-Reggiano can be used either alone or mixed with grated Pecorino Romano for a slightly more robust flavor.

Pecorino Romano: A hard cheese made from sheep's milk. It has a sharp, salty flavor and is excellent as a grating cheese (mix with grated Parmigiano-Reggiano if a milder taste is desired) or as a table cheese.

Pecorino siciliano: A sheep's milk cheese from Sicily. It is flavored with black peppercorns and is a very hard, piquant cheese.

Provolone: A cheese made from cow's milk. When young (2 to 3 months) it is quite delicate and mild. Once aged, it becomes a much harder, sharper cheese. It has a stringy (layered) texture.

Ricotta piemontese: A soft, very mild cheese that is made with the whey from cow's milk. It is excellent as a table cheese and for cooking or baking. It does not keep long, so keep it refrigerated and use it within two or three days.
In several recipes I say to squeeze the excess liquid from the ricotta. This is done by placing the cheese in some cheesecloth, gathering the cloth up around the ricotta, and twisting it tightly.

Ricotta romana: The same as the ricotta piemontese but made with the whey from sheep's milk.

Romano: A cow's milk cheese made in the United States. It is a hard, strongly flavored cheese that is used for grating.

Scamorza: A semi-hard cheese from Southern Italy that is made from either cow's milk or a mixture of cow's and sheep's milk. It comes tied like a little bundle and is excellent as either a table or cooking cheese.

Scamorza affumicata: The same as scamorza but smoked.

Stracchino: A very soft, mild cheese from Lombardy. It is made from cow's milk and is used as both a table and cooking cheese.

Taleggio: A soft, cow's milk cheese from Lombardy. It has a slightly acidic flavor and is good both as a cooking cheese and as a table cheese.

Toma: A cheese from Val d'Aosta, Piedmont or Savoy that is made from whole or partially skimmed cow's milk. The younger cheese is strongly flavored, while the more aged cheese is sharp and salty.

Chicken (Pollo)

Buy fresh, not frozen, chicken because it is more succulent and tender. Cook within two days of purchasing it. Before preparing the chicken, rinse it thoroughly with cold water. Keep a separate cutting board for chicken and wash it and any utensils used to cut the chicken—as well as your hands—immediately after use. This minimizes the danger of infection by salmonella bacteria.

Whole chickens come in various weights, and some are more suited to certain preparations than others. Here is a guide:
Broiling chickens (broilers) weigh 1½ to 2½ pounds.
Frying chickens weigh 3 to 3½ pounds.
Boiling chickens weigh 4 to 5 pounds and are meatier.
Roasting chickens also weigh 4 to 5 pounds, are meaty and have quite a bit of fat.

Cream (Panna)

Cream is called for in many of the recipes. Heavy cream will produce the richest, most flavorful result. For a lighter preparation use light cream, and if you must be diet-conscious, use half-and-half; the reduction time on these sauces may be longer in order to thicken the sauce.

Eggs (Uova)

Always use the freshest eggs available and do not keep them long after purchase. Store eggs tightly covered in the refrigerator (the shells are porous and allow the passage of air into the egg). When cooking and baking, it is best to use eggs at room temperature, so remove them from the refrigerator at least 30 minutes ahead of time. Buy large grade 'A' brown or white eggs.

To boil eggs properly, place the eggs in a saucepan and cover them with cold water and a dash of vinegar. Bring the water to a boil and cook for 15 minutes. Remove the eggs from the water and place them in ice water for 5 minutes. Peel immediately or store unpeeled in the refrigerator.

Fat and Lard (Strutto E Lardo)

Rendered lard or pork fat is excellent for roasting and sautéing. Prosciutto fat can also be rendered for an even more flavorful fat, as can chicken fat, pancetta and bacon.

To render, place the lard or fat in a roasting pan in a slow (300 degree) oven. Allow the fat to melt slowly, and pour it off as it does. When the process is completed, only crispy pieces of meat or skin will be left. Store the rendered fat in a tightly sealed jar in the refrigerator.

In one recipe, I specify to blanch pork fat. To do this, bring a large pot of cold water to a boil, add ample salt and then add the strip of fat to the water. Do not let the water return to a boil. Let the fat blanch for 3 minutes. Remove it from the water, plunge it into ice water until it is completely cooled and pat dry with paper towels.

Fish (Pesce)

Always buy the freshest fish and shellfish available, preferably those varieties that are indigenous to your area. When buying fish, it should smell fresh, not fishy; the skin should be shiny and the flesh firm to the touch. If buying a whole fish, the eyes should be clear, the scales intact, the flesh firm and the gills red with blood. Have your fish merchant clean the fish for you. If a whole fish is required, leave on the head and tail. If you need fillets, ask for the head, tail and bones and use these to make your fish stock.

Cook fish only until it is opaque and the flesh flakes. The cooking time for a whole fish is about 10 minutes per inch of thickness (measure it at its thickest point). This time, however, is not an absolute, so test the fish as it cooks. Fillets will take an amazingly brief time to cook.

When purchasing clams, mussels and oysters, the shells should be tightly closed, and they should smell fresh. Wash them under cold running water, using a stiff-bristled brush to scrub them. Mussels also have a "beard" that must be removed. The beard consists of several strands of fiber that protrude from the seam of the shell and serve to attach the mussel to rocks, etc. Remove the beard by giving it a strong pull, or pulling it up and out.

Cook mussels, clams and oysters only until the shells open. If they are particularly large, they may be cooked an additional minute or two.

If you purchase scallops in the shells, treat them as you would clams, etc. Usually, however, one purchases them already shelled. In this case, the scallops should be white or pink, fresh-smelling and firm to the touch. Clean the scallops by rinsing them in cold water and pulling off the small piece of muscle on the side (it will protrude slightly and be of a different texture). Cook scallops only until they are opaque.

You will most likely buy frozen shrimp (size 16×20) which must be thawed either in the refrigerator or under cold running water. If called for in the recipe, clean the shrimp by peeling off the shells, leaving the tails on. Save the shells to use in your fish stock or fish sauce. If desired, slice down the back of the shrimp and remove the intestine. Cook shrimp only until opaque.

These days one usually buys squid already cleaned. It should be porcelain-white or pink, firm and fresh-smelling. If you do buy whole squid, either fresh or frozen, you will have to clean it before cooking. To do this, pull to remove the head. Pull out the ink sac and cartilage and peel the dark outer skin from the body. Rinse it inside and out with cold water. You will be left with a clean, white sack that can be stuffed whole or sliced into rings or chunks. Pull the eyes from the tentacles, wash the tentacles, and use them in your preparation. Cook squid until it is opaque and tender.

Purchase lobsters that are quite lively. The smaller (younger) ones will be more tender than the larger (older) ones. To boil a lobster, bring a large pot of cold water to a boil. Add the whole lobster head first to the pot and bring the water back to a boil. From that point, boil the lobster for 6 minutes per pound.

Flour (Farina)

I always use unbleached white flour for baking. All-purpose flour may be used in all other preparations. Flour can be measured by weight, using a small kitchen scale (which is more accurate) or in dry-measure measuring cups.

Fruit (Frutta)

Use only fruit that is in season and ripe. Fruit should be fragrant when ripe and have firm, sweet flesh. These days with insecticides, it is best to peel fruit before eating it. When using fruit in a cooked dish, it's better if the fruit is on the firm side rather than overripe.

Herbs (Odori) and Spices (Aromi)

When possible use fresh herbs because nothing surpasses their taste. Fresh herbs are now available in many supermarkets and produce markets, but they are very easy to grow, either outside or inside. The herbs most commonly used in Italian cooking are rosemary, oregano, basil, sage and tarragon. If using dried herbs, check their potency by smelling them. They should be aromatic. Be careful in using dried herbs because they will usually be stronger and sharper in flavor than fresh herbs. Keep dried herbs tightly covered and stored in a cool, dry place. Preserve fresh herbs by wrapping them in damp towels and keeping them in the refrigerator. To keep fresh parsley (I prefer the Italian flat-leafed variety) and basil, keep them in the refrigerator with their stems in water. If possible, cover the leaves with a damp towel.

Spices also should be smelled to make sure that they are fragrant. Store spices tightly covered in a cool dry place.

Anise (Anice): A small oblong seed used in baking and in soup preparations. It is used crushed or whole and has a pleasant licorice flavor. Also called fennel seed.

Basil (Basilico): Fresh basil has broad, bright green leaves. It has a delicate, fragrant flavor and is wonderful in a wide array of summer dishes.

Dried basil is very strong with a slightly bitter taste, so use it sparingly.

Bay leaves or laurel (Lauro): This is a dried leaf that is dark green in color and highly aromatic. It is an essential ingredient in stocks, sauces, soups, marinades and meat roasts.

Capers (Capperi): The buds of the caper bush. They come preserved in brine or salt and must be rinsed very well before using. I prefer to rinse a quantity of capers and store them in dry white wine in the refrigerator. The wine gives them a milder, sweeter flavor. Capers add a special piquant accent to many dishes. I prefer the larger capers.

Garlic (Aglio): Only use fresh garlic. The bulb (head) of garlic should be plump, tightly packed and firm. When sliced, the cloves (individual pieces) should be highly fragrant. The more finely one slices or chops garlic the more flavor it imparts. In several recipes, I refer to pressing garlic. This imparts the strongest flavor and is done by using either a garlic press or a mortar and pestle.

Juniper berries: A fragrant, dried, blue-black berry that is used in marinades and in meat preparations. Available in specialty food shops.

Nutmeg (Noce moscata): A roasted nut about ½ inch in diameter. The more readily available form is ground, but if you can, go to a specialty food store and purchase the whole nut. Use a fine hand-grater or special nutmeg grater to grate the nut when needed. This will give the most flavor. Nutmeg is excellent in baking, as well as in sauces and meat and chicken dishes.

Oregano (Origano): Fresh Italian oregano has a small, round, green leaf and a delicate flavor. Dried oregano has a strong, sharp flavor, so use it judiciously. Dried oregano is excellent sprinkled over slices of fresh tomatoes and mozzarella that have been dressed with extra virgin olive oil.

Pepper (Pepe): If you do not have a peppermill, buy one because the taste of freshly ground pepper far surpasses that of pre-ground. Freshly grind both black and white peppercorns. White pepper is less pungent but hotter than the black and will not add color to a white sauce. Peppercorns are available in supermarkets and specialty food shops.

Red Pepper (Peperoncino): When possible, buy the whole, dried red peppers and cut off small pieces as needed, otherwise crushed pods may be used.

Rosemary (Rosmarino): A long, thin, highly fragrant leaf. The fresh leaf is dark green and more subtly flavored than the darker dried leaf. If you use the dried rosemary in making a sauce, blanch it first. Rosemary goes well with meat, chicken, fish and vegetables.

Saffron (Zafferano): This is the dried stamen of the crocus flower. The strands are long and thin and the color should be red with only a little yellow. It is a very expensive spice, so use it judiciously. Be careful not to use too much saffron as it will give a medicinal taste; a small amount goes a long way and gives a mild, bittersweet flavor and yellow color to foods. Saffron is also used in breadbaking.

Sage (Salvia): Only use fresh sage because the ground, dried herb gives a musty flavor. The leaves are grayish green, long and slightly fuzzy. Sage is wonderful in soups, sauces, marinades and roasts.

Tarragon (Dragoncello): A long, thin, olive green leaf that has a wonderful delicate flavor. The dried leaf is darker and slightly bitter, so use it judiciously.

Thyme (Timo): Fresh thyme is much more delicately flavored than the dried herb. If using the dried herb, use the leaf—not the powder. Thyme is excellent in stocks, soups and roasts.

Turmeric (Curcuma): This is purchased in ground form. Turmeric has a very mild, sweet flavor and imparts a strong yellow color to foods.

Meat (Carne)

Buy only the freshest meats and game, and have them cut and dressed as necessary by your butcher. Have him give you the bones and scraps to use in making stock.

Cured meats and sausages play an important role in Italian cooking, so acquaint yourself with the many varieties and special flavors.

Pancetta: This is a cured pork much like bacon. It has a higher meat content than bacon, however, and it is cured in salt and pepper. It also has a more delicate flavor, and for this reason, I prefer it for cooking. Bacon can, however, be substituted for pancetta. Purchase pancetta in Italian grocery stores or specialty food shops.

Prosciutto: Imported prosciutto is, of course, preferable to domestic, but our domestic variety is a fine substitute. When buying prosciutto, make sure that it does not have much fat and is a pinkish red color, not dark red. Have the prosciutto sliced paper-thin and ask the grocer for extra prosciutto fat (the scraps from the sliced meat); take this home and render it. If you can get the bone, too, use it for making soups.

Besides being used in cooking, prosciutto is excellent eaten with fruits like melon and figs or alone on a slice of crusty, coarse-textured Italian bread with olive oil sprinkled on top. Eat it as a sandwich with slices of salty focaccia (pizza bread) as the Italians do.

Sausages (Salsiccie): There are a variety of Italian sausages, but the most common are the sweet and hot sausages of southern Italy. I have used sweet sausages in the recipes in this book. In some of the recipes, I say to remove the sausage from its casing; do so by splitting the casing with a knife and removing the contents.

Salami: This is a name for cured meats such as mortadella and coppa. The meats are used in appetizers, cooked dishes, salads, sandwiches or as meals in themselves. Find a good Italian grocer for a variety.

Bresaola: This is a salt-and air-dried cured beef. Slice it thinly as with prosciutto and eat it sprinkled with extra virgin olive oil for an appetizer or light meal.

Nuts (Noci)

I use nuts extensively in cooking, so I like to keep a supply of almonds, walnuts and pine nuts on hand. Pistachios and hazelnuts come in handy, too. Store nuts in a cool, dry place in tightly sealed small amounts. They may also be frozen with excellent results.

Pine nuts are small, oblong, delicately flavored nuts from Italy. There is a Chinese variety that is shorter and plumper but with the same delicate flavor. Walnuts may be substituted for a similar flavor. Pine nuts can be purchased in any Italian grocery or specialty food shop.

Nuts are often toasted to bring out their flavor. To do so, place the nuts in a heavy-bottomed skillet and toast them over low heat or in a slow oven. Toss them continuously to keep them from burning. Once lightly browned, remove the nuts from the pan and let cool.

Olives (Olive)

When I specify black olives in cooking, I am referring to the Italian Gaeta olives or the Greek Kalamata. They should be firm, fleshy and sweet.

Two other types that I use often are the bitter Sicilian olives and the large, salty green olives. The Sicilian olives are small, black and wrinkled and are preserved in olive oil and red pepper. They have a strong flavor and are excellent with antipasti, cured meats, cheeses and bread.

The large, plump, green olives are excellent in antipasti and salads or in cooked preparations. Buy them with the pit in (not the pimiento-stuffed variety) and remove the pit if you are using them in cooking.

Olive Oil (Olio d'Oliva)

Good olive oil is essential to Italian cooking. The lighter imported virgin olive oils are readily available in supermarkets. This is an excellent all-purpose olive oil and is the one to be used in the recipes in this book, unless extra virgin olive oil is specified.

The extra virgin olive oils are fruitier (greener), more full-flavored and heavier than the virgin olive oils. The flavor and color of the oil will vary according to where it is made because not all olives are alike. Find an Italian grocer or a specialty food shop that carries a nice variety and experiment. These extra virgin olive oils are used in preparations in which the flavor of the oil is intrinsic to the overall flavor of the dish: salads, antipasti, Pasta alla Primavera, Spaghetti Aglio e Olio, Bruschette, etc. During the summer when ripe, fresh tomatoes are available, try sprinkling some extra virgin olive oil on a thick slice of coarse Italian bread and topping it with a thick slice of tomato and a sprinkle of salt. Delicious!

Pasta

Buy a good imported dried pasta instead of the domestic dried pasta. Several brands are now imported (DeCecco, San Martino, Agnesi, Martelli, etc.) and are available in many large supermarkets. If you have access to good quality fresh pasta, I would suggest using it occasionally with the lighter sauces or in "brodo" (broth or consommé). However, to my taste, the dried pasta usually has a better flavor and texture than the fresh.

Pasta comes in a seemingly endless variety of shapes and sizes. Try various shapes but remember that certain shapes are better for certain preparations. The tubular and shell shapes, for example, are most often used when the pasta is meant to hold or contain the sauce, as in cheesy pasta dishes, baked pastas, etc. Use the more interesting shapes (fusilli, ruote, etc.) to make beautiful and fun pasta salads.

Agnolotti: Half-moons of stuffed pasta. They are traditionally stuffed with meat or a sweet butternut squash mixture, but this can change according to one's imagination.

Bucatini: A long, thin macaroni that is hollow inside. It is excellent with fish-based sauces.

Capelli d' Angelo (Angel's hair): The thinnest spaghettini. A very fine, delicate pasta.

Ditali: Very short tubes of pasta (more like pieces of a tube).

Ditalini: Even smaller ditali. These are used in soups and broths.

Farfalle (Butterflies): A butterfly-shaped pasta that has little ridges along the edges.

Fettuccine: A broad, flat noodle typically used in cream sauces.

Lasagne: The broadest flat noodle with either a curly or a smooth edge. It is used in baked dishes.

Linguine: A long, thin pasta much like spaghetti but thicker and flattened (but not flat). I often use this instead of vermicelli or spaghetti.

Lumachelle: Short, curved lengths of grooved tubular pasta that looks like someone cut off from the tube and left the curve.

Mostaccioli: Similar to penne but with grooves. Also called penne rigate.

Penne: One-inch-long or shorter tubular pasta that is cut on the diagonal.

Ravioli: Stuffed squares of pasta. The filling depends on one's imagination.

Rigatoni: Large, grooved tubular pasta, two to three inches in length. The wider tubes are called "Occhi di lupo" or wolf's eyes.

Ruote: Wheel-shaped pasta (with spokes). These are fun to use in pasta salads.

Semi di mellone and Semi di cicoria: Tiny, seedlike pasta that is used in broths.

Spaghetti: The long, thin pasta with which most Americans are familiar.

Spaghettini: A thinner form of spaghetti.

Tagliatelle: Same as fettuccine but not as wide.

Tortellini and Tortelloni: Small, doughnut-shaped pastas. The tortellini are usually stuffed with a meat and cheese mixture, while the tortelloni, which are fatter, are usually stuffed with a spinach and ricotta cheese mixture or a sweet butternut squash mixture.

Vermicelli: A long, thin pasta like spaghetti but thicker.

Ziti: Long, smooth tubes of pasta. They come in various lengths and widths.

To cook pasta, bring an abundant amount of water (the pasta should not be crowded) to a boil and add a generous amount of salt (kosher salt dissolves better). Add the pasta to the water and stir to keep it from sticking together. (When cooking lasagne noodles, add a little olive oil to the water to keep the noodles from sticking together, which they do quite readily.) Cover the pot and return the water to a boil. Continue to cook the pasta at a boil, stirring often, until it is *al dente* (i.e., softened but still with a slight firmness or bite. Test for the right degree of doneness by biting into a piece of pasta.) This will take anywhere from about 6 minutes for the thinner pasta to 8 or 9 minutes for the thicker varieties. Fresh pasta will take 2 to 3 minutes, and stuffed, fresh pasta about 5 minutes.

Once the pasta is cooked, drain it immediately in a colander and transfer it to a warm serving bowl or platter. Add the sauce, toss and serve immediately. For certain preparations, you will cook the pasta briefly with its sauce before serving.

A word on serving sizes. Two ounces is the standard portion of pasta to be served as a first course. Double this portion if the pasta is served as a main course. The amounts will, however, depend on one's appetite: There are many people who can eat 4 ounces as a first course.

Polenta (Cornmeal)

Polenta is a staple of Northern Italy and is eaten, much as are rice and pasta, as a first course. It is also used as an accompaniment to strongly flavored dishes.

It is best to use imported Italian polenta, which can be found in Italian grocery stores or specialty food shops. American stone-ground yellow cornmeal may also be used with fairly good results. Store polenta tightly covered in a cool, dry place.

Rice (Riso)

When making Italian rice dishes, use imported Arborio rice, a short, white rice that comes from Northern Italy. If you cannot find Arborio rice in any Italian grocery or specialty food store, other brands may be substituted; the result, however, will not be the same. I have found that short-grained brown rice is the best substitute for taste and texture.

Tomato Paste (Conserva di Pomodoro)

Tomato paste is used to accent and heighten the flavor of tomatoes in sauces (it also thickens the sauce). When possible, buy the imported tubes of tomato paste, which allow you to use only what you need and then store the remainder easily. If you use the canned paste, freeze the extra paste in tablespoon amounts and use as needed.

Truffles (Tartufi)

This is a fungus that grows near the roots of shrub oak or beech trees. The truffle can be about the size and shape of a golf ball or larger and is either black (from France) or white (from Italy). Keep truffles stored in raw rice in a tightly sealed container in a cool, dry place.

Truffles have a slightly unpleasant odor when raw, but once cooked they lend a very special flavor to foods.

Vegetables (Ortaggi e Legumi)

Use only fresh vegetables and those that are in season. (Frozen peas are the only frozen vegetable that I find acceptable.) Vegetables should be firm or crisp. Avoid vegetables that have begun to shrivel or have brown spots on them. Leafy vegetables should have leaves that are richly colored, not yellow or brown, and are crisp, not wilted. The smaller, younger vegetables will be sweeter than the larger, more mature ones.

To keep leafy vegetables crisp, store them in damp towels or in a damp pillowcase in the refrigerator. Store root vegetables in a cool, dry place. Use vegetables shortly after purchase.

I often say to "blanch" a vegetable. I do this to preserve its color and to cook it only until tender or *al dente*. Bring a large pot of water to a boil. Salt the water and add the cut vegetable (always do white vegetables first) or put the vegetable in a wire basket and put this into the water. Bring the water almost to a boil, but do not let it boil. Cook (blanch) the vegetable just until tender (it should have a firmness to it). Drain and "shock" in ice water until the vegetable is completely cooled, then drain and pat dry.

Dried Beans (Fagioli Secchi): These are a wonderful food and an excellent source of protein. There is quite a variety of dried beans, so experiment with the various colors, shapes and flavors. Use them in both hot and cold dishes.

Many Italian recipes call for cannellini beans, which are white beans that look much like red kidney beans. Ceci or chickpeas or garbanzo beans are a nut colored bean with a delicate, nutty flavor. Lentils are a flat, dark green or brown, dried legume.

Beans can be purchased dried or already cooked and canned. I prefer to buy the dried beans because they are superior in taste and texture to the canned beans (the latter are also cooked with a good deal of salt). Simply sort (to remove any foreign objects) and rinse the beans, and then soak them overnight in an abundant amount of cold water. The next day, drain, cover with cold water and bring to a boil. Add a little salt to the water and cook the beans at a slow boil until tender (from 1 hour for cannellini beans to 2 or 3 hours for ceci beans).

Mushrooms (Funghi): A variety of mushrooms are now available in the better markets. If you can find them, try fresh chanterelles and morels; they can be used alone or mixed with domestic champignon mushrooms. Several of the recipes in this book call for the Italian porcini mushrooms. These come in dried form, are long and flat and are light brown in color. They give a distinctive, almost smoky or woody flavor to certain dishes. Soak the mushrooms in tepid water for 1 to 1½ hours before using. The porcini are also excellent mixed with fresh mushrooms and will give an added strength, as well as a different texture to the dish. Keep the dried mushrooms tightly covered and store in a cool, dry place.

Never use canned or frozen mushrooms.

Mancini peppers: This is a brand of canned roasted red peppers that have an excellent taste and texture—they are sweet and succulent. You may, of course, roast your own peppers by charring the skin completely either over a flame or in a very hot oven. Once the skins are blackened, put the peppers in a paper bag, close the bag tightly and let sit for 5 minutes. Remove them from the bag, peel off the skins under cold running water, pull out the stem and remove the seeds.

Potatoes (Patate): I refer to "ricing" potatoes in one of the recipes. This is done with a potato ricer. The cooked, peeled potato passes through the holes in the ricer and comes out in strands.

Tomatoes (Pomodori): Many of the recipes call for peeled and seeded Italian plum tomatoes. I use the cans of imported whole tomatoes that are packed in their own juices. These are already peeled and can be easily seeded by cutting them in half and scooping out the seeds with your finger or passing them through a mesh strainer. Fresh plum tomatoes can also be used when in season. Blanch them briefly to allow you to easily peel the skins. Slice them in half and gently squeeze out the seeds.

Vinegar (Aceto)

There are many types of vinegar, but I use a red wine vinegar more than any other. Buy a full-bodied Italian brand. I also use balsamic vinegar often. This is an Italian vinegar that has been aged for a longer period than a regular vinegar. It is brown in color and has a very special taste. Purchase balsamic vinegar in Italian groceries or specialty food shops. There are many flavored vinegars that you can try in dressings and sauces.

Wine (Vino)

A brief note on cooking wines: Always use a good wine for cooking because it will impart its flavor to the preparations.

A FINAL NOTE ON TECHNIQUE: Reducing a sauce means to cook a sauce, usually over high heat, until it has thickened. As the sauce boils or simmers, the liquid evaporates and the sauce reduces to a thicker state. To "nape" a food with a sauce means to carefully cover it with the sauce.

When sautéing a preparation, use a pan large enough to comfortably hold all the ingredients, i.e., the ingredients should easily have contact with the bottom of the pan and, thus, the heat source. If you do not have a pan large enough, simply use two pans, dividing the ingredients between them.

A FINAL NOTE

The A-House in Provincetown, a restaurant owned by art collector Reggie Cabral, where Ciro once worked as a waiter, was, in its early years, an important club for jazz players and entertainers. Kay Ballard, May Barns, Wally Cox, Jerry Mulligan and Zoot Simms all played there. They would all come to CIRO & SAL'S to meet with the other artists of the town.

The Provincetown Playhouse was equally important for actors and actresses, and they too gathered at the restaurant. In later years, Helen Hayes and Truman Capote were among those who visited CIRO & SAL'S.

The artists would congregate around the family table next to the open kitchen, where they could be part of Ciro and Sal's activities in the kitchen (and vice versa). They would stay the night to discuss politics and art, argue, play music and, of course, eat. The family table became the focal point of the restaurant, and Provincetown's most important gathering spot for artists.

Here are some of the artists, writers, musicians and other influential personalities who have passed through the restaurant's doors:

CINEMA AND THEATER
Truman Capote
Divine
Helen Hayes
Andy Warhol
John Waters

COLLECTORS
Reggie Cabral
Berta Walker, owner of the Graham Gallery in New York City
Hudson Walker, head of the Walker Foundation in Minneapolis
Bill Brill

PAINTERS AND SCULPTORS

Courtney Allen
Mary Cecil Allen
Yvonne Anderson
William C. Arthur
Mary Ascher
Elise Asher
Milton Avery
Susan Baker
Wallace Bassford
Robert Beauchamp
Janice Tworkov Biala
Deane Bloomberg
Betty Bodian
Varujan Boghosian
Henry Botkin
Paul Bowen
Anne Brigadier
Gandy Brodie
Fritz Bultman
Peter Busa
Victor Candell
Mihran Chobanian
Carmen Cicero
Arthur Cohen
Edward Corbett
Victor DeCarlo
Nanno de Groot
Salvatore DelDeo
Morgan Dennis
Vivian DePinna
Edwin Dickinson
Al DiLauro
Harvey Dodd
Ray Elman

Harry Engel
Edwin Reeves Euler
William Evaul
Jerry Farnsworth
Remo Farruggio
Richard Florsheim
Jim Forsberg
Willim Freed
Cy Fried
Martin Friedman
Sideo Fromboluti
James Gahagan
Jan Gelb
Ed Giobbi
Sidney Gordin
Adolf Gottlieb
John Gregory
John Grillo
Red Grooms
Mimi Gross Grooms
Chaim Gross
James Hansen
Lily Harmon
Charles Lloyd Heins
Henry Hensche
Hans Hofmann
Gerrit Hondius
Budd Hopkins
Jane Horner
John Hultberg
Robert Douglas Hunter
Angelo Ippolito
Al Jaffe
Hank Jensen

Marit Jensen
Joyce Johnson
Lester Johnson
Mervin Jules
Wolf Kahn
Alex Katz
Lila Katzen
Jack Kearney
Yeffe Kimball
Franz Kline
Karl Knaths
Eric Koch
Paul Koch
Jane Kogan
Stanley Kunitz
Bailey LaForce
Sharli Powers Land
Jack Larned
Blanche Lazzel
James Lechay
Irving Lefson
Mary Lefson
Lucy L'Engle
William L'Engle
Al Leslie
Peter Macara
Bruce McKain
George McNeil
Philip Malicoat
Leo Manso
Irving Marantz
Michael Marantz
Daniel Marcus
Marcia Marcus
Boris Margo
Herman Maril
Joel Meyerowitz
Ross Moffett
Edith Morrison
Robert Motherwell
Seong Moy

Jan Muller
John Noble
Claes Thure Oldenburg
Edmund S. Oppenheim
Stephen Pace
Jim Parr
Richard Pepitone
Chester Pfeiffer
Ian Pinkerson
Vollian Rann
Paul Resika
Mischa Richter
Larry Rivers
Romanos Risk
Phil Roeber
Michael Rogofsky
Umberto Romano
Judith Rothchild
Marc Rothko
Howie Schneider
Ben Shahn
Sidney Simon
Arlie Sinaiko
Richard E. Smith
Raphael Soyer
Maurice Sterne
Myron Stout
Frederick Tasch
Sabina Teichman
Bob Thompson
Selina Trieff
Jack Tworkov
Janice Tworkov
Elspeth Vevers
Tabitha Vevers
Tony Vevers
Ione Walker
Peter Watts
Daniel Weisberg
Ray Martan Wells
John Whorf

Sol Wilson
Marjorie Windust
Ben Wolf
Cleveland Woodward

Taro Yamamoto
George Yater
William Zorach

MUSICIANS
Kay Ballard
Kay Barnes

Wally Cox
Zoot Simms

WRITERS AND POETS
Keith Althaus
Eddie Bonetti
Olga Broumas
R. V. Cassill
Gregory Corso
Joseph DeRocco
Annie Dillard
John Dos Passos
Alan Dugan
B. H. Freidman
Susan Glaspell
Louise Gluck
Hutchins Hapgood
Cecil Hemley
Denis Johnson
E. J. Kahn, Jr.
Terry Kahn
Weldon Kees

Harry Kemp
Stephen Kinzer
Stanley Kunitz
Norman Mailer
Peter Manso
Hilary Masters
Christie Morris
Mary Oliver
Eugene O'Neill
Jayne Anne Phillips
Irving Sandler
Roger Skillings
Mark Strand
Arturo Vivante
Mary Heaton Vorse
Alec Wilkinson
Edmund Wilson

INDEX